Irish Gardens

A vista of Mount Stewart, the Marchioness of Londonderry's great garden in Co. Down.

Irish Gardens

Text by
EDWARD HYAMS

Photographs by
WILLIAM MacQUITTY

ERRATA

Plate facing page 56. The caption should read: "Ilnacullin, the unique Italianate garden in Glengariff Bay".

Plate facing page 144. The caption should read: "Glenveagh, the remote and beautiful garden maintained by Mr. Henry McIlhenny in Co. Donegal".

Pages 78 and 80. For Major and the Hon. Mrs. Ball read Major and the Hon. Mrs. Bell.

The lines on page 69 are not in sequence. The sentence at the foot of page 68 is continued on line 5 of page 69, and the first four lines on page 69 should start a new paragraph at the foot of this page.

ιgazine

THE MACMILLAN COMPANY : NEW YORK

3

Published in the United States by The Macmillan Company 1967

Library of Congress number: 67-12795

Printed in West Germany

Foreword

by Daniel J. Foley

former editor of Horticulture Magazine

Ireland has long been a source of delight to discerning American travelers. Not the least of its charms are the lovely gardens. Even in this age of easy travel, however, not everyone can visit all the gardens of his choice; but enjoying man-made landscapes is made possible by vivid writing and heightened by skilled photography, giving a new dimension to armchair gardening.

Few small countries offer more allure than does Ireland with its gardens great and small. Endowed by nature with rare attributes, set amid the untamed beauty of lakes and mountains, protected by warm Gulf Stream winds, the diaphanous light in this seagirt land etches borders and beds, gilds trees and shrubs, and limns architecture with an amazing sharpness. Visitors recall with great joy the greenest of green lawns and the brilliance of endless floral displays, infinite in variety, many of which are pictured in this book.

By virtue of its location — the westernmost of large European islands — Ireland is a place of solitude. Though the Irish have always revealed a love of nature in their poetry, song, stone sculpture, metalcraft, illuminated manuscripts, and, perhaps more especially, in the charming place names of their villages, it remained for those beyond their borders to design and develop most of the notable private gardens that today flourish in Ireland. In the eighteenth century and well into the nineteenth, the English gentry built great houses and created gardens truly worthy of their settings. Rare exotic treasures, gathered by intrepid plant hunters from South American jungles and Asian mountain valleys, rooted and flourished in the wet mild climate of Ireland to an extent not realized elsewhere in the British Isles.

Edward Hyams has drawn on his vast knowledge of garden art to interpret for us the rare charm of Irish gardens. The superb photography of William MacQuitty has added luster, tone, and quality to this utterly delightful book. For those who have visited Ireland, it will recall that green land's myriad beauties; for those unable to travel, this book will serve as a well-conducted garden tour, offering new inspiration and pleasure in green things growing, and in the men and women who have created and nurtured these unforgettable gardens.

Salem, Massachussetts

Acknowledgments

Acknowledgments and ·thanks are due to the following authors and owners of copyright for permission to reproduce copyright material: *Country Life* for extracts from an article by G. C. Taylor published in *Country Life*; the Department of Agriculture and Fisheries, Dublin, for extract from "Botanic Gardens: Origin, History and Development" by J. W. Besant, published in the *Department of Agriculture Journal*; Mr Lanning Roper for extracts from his contribution to *Mount Usher, Wicklow*; the Royal Horticultural Society and Dr R. H. Fletcher, Regis Keeper of the Royal Botanic Garden, Edinburgh, Mr Lanning Roper and Mr G. S. Thomas for extracts from their articles published in the Royal Horticultural Society *Journal*; the Royal Horticultural Society for extracts from an article by Earl Annesley published in the Royal Horticultural Society *Journal*; the National Trust for extracts from their guides to the National Trust properties of Rowallane and Mount Stewart; Mr Robert Walpole for extracts by Mr E. H. Walpole and Sir Frederick Moore from *Mount Usher, Wicklow*.

Technical Data. William MacQuitty used two Asahi Pentax cameras, models S3 and SV, each fitted with Asahi Pentax CdS clip-on exposure meters. One was loaded with Kodak Tri-X black and white film and the other either with Kodachrome II or Kodak High Speed Ektachrome film. He used three Asahi Pentax lenses: 28 mm, F. 3.5 Super-Takumar; 55 mm, F. 1.8 Super-Takumar; and 135 mm, F. 3.5 Super-Takumar.

At Mount Stewart all the traditional garden styles are represented in a single work of art.

Contents

Mount Stewart. The Harp of Ireland in topiary, a garden art since 1000 B.C.

List of Colour Plates

Mount Stewart. The living arcade is clipped in *Cupressus macrocarpa*.

1
Origins of the Irish Garden

No people excels in all the arts: the Irish, and perhaps this is true of the Celtic-speaking peoples in general, with their remarkable genius for literature and for music, succeed less often in the visual arts, and very rarely in architecture: it is not, as we say nowadays, their "thing". Moreover they were, in the past, primarily pastoral rather than agricultural people, coming later to an interest in the cultivation of plants than did the other Europeans. Now the two parts of gardening can be called architectural and botanical; it is, therefore, no wonder that the Irish were not among the early gardening peoples. Moreover, the history of Ireland is wanting in that chapter which saw the introduction of gardening to England: the Roman conquest of England was never extended to Ireland; as a consequence, Ireland had none of those Roman villa gardens of the kind described by the younger Pliny in his letters which, in the second and third centuries, were represented in England and especially in parts of the south. It is, therefore, probable that the first gardens in Ireland were made in the seventh and eighth centuries of our era, about the monasteries and other religious establishments founded by Breton and Northumbrian missionaries and which became the glory of early medieval Ireland, the Ireland of saints and scholars.

The monastery gardens of Europe in general had their origin in the tiny gardens of the early medieval hermits of Italy. These solitary teachers made their hermitages among the ruins of ancient Roman villas and palaces and, in some patch of ground among the fallen columns and capitals, planted salads, pot herbs and medicinal herbs, and perhaps a few flowers, among them violets, roses and lilies. It may well be that in tracing this practice to the influence of St. Augustine, Georgina Masson is right: in her *Italian Gardens* (Thames and Hudson, London, 1961) she tells us that following the Platonic tradition—and thus helping to carry it forward into a later age—Augustine did his teaching in a garden at Hippo which had been given to him for that purpose by a rich friend. The hermits of a later period, then, following that literally august example, made gardens among the ruins of

Rome and other Italian cities, in which to teach those who came to them for guidance.

Nor was it only this ancient and pleasant practice that they borrowed from the ancients: they probably tried to reproduce, on a miserably reduced scale, of course, features of the great Roman gardens of the past. As a consequence, when monasteries began to be founded, when the eremitic movement became cenobitic and had had time to grow rich, the monastery garden tended to be a recreation of the old Roman gardens. St. Benedict planted a rose garden about his grotto near the ruins of Nero's villa at Subiaco; he planted another garden when he left that retreat to found the first monastic order of western Europe at Cassino. The early monastery gardens of Italy, and the later ones of Ireland, were very small, and their purpose was the cultivation of pot herbs, salads, medicinal herbs and a few flowers. But the parterres in which they did so were edged with clipped box in the Roman manner. And, centuries later, enriched and able to do something grander, they still recalled the Roman models so that, when, in 1070, the Abbey of Cassino was rebuilt, the garden was described as "a paradise in the Roman tradition".

The first element in the Irish garden is then an ancient Roman one; can be traced, although only vaguely and generally, back to the Platonic academy; and was carried forward by the monkish gardeners into the period of the Renaissance and later. There is, of course, no surviving Irish garden which is a pure example of this ancient style. What does survive is a tradition of design in certain parts of some Irish gardens, and that not directly but by way of a second influence, that of the Italian Humanist garden which reached Ireland from Tuscany by way of Western Europe in general, and of England, and after a long delay.

If the Renaissance began as an attempt to recover the ancient learning and the arts of Greece and Rome, it soon changed its nature: the past remained the inspiration but ceased to be a model to be merely copied. Under its inspiration, men working in its spirit, or in a new version of its spirit, created not copies, but something new. This they did in the art of the gardens as well as in the other arts. There grew up, between the fourteenth and seventeenth centuries in Italy, two different schools of garden design and planting: the Tuscan, equated by Miss Masson with Humanism, and originally inspired and even, though unsuccessfully, practised by Petrarch; and that of the great Renaissance garden designers of Rome and its environs. Both styles were in due course incorporated into the garden design styles of Western Europe. The famous Twickenham garden of Alexander Pope was, in spirit and to some extent even in design, a Humanist garden. The style reached Ireland by way of England, and very late, but not too late to add a valuable element to the Irish garden. The other great Italian style, Roman Renaissance, is very much grander, more stately, makes use of buildings, walls and statues with more freedom, and is, as a rule, on a vaster and more pretentious scale. That element also is to be found in the Irish garden.

I should make it clear that there is, in the use of these elements in the Irish garden, no

Eucryphia, in all its species and varieties, is the late summer glory of Irish gardens.

question of chronological order, of style imposed on style in succession. Nothing of the kind; the various elements, traditions, styles all survive, have their ups and downs, and their periods of eclipse or of fashion. The Humanist, or the Renaissance, style is from time to time recalled when there is a reaction against some later fashion in garden design and it is used to check excesses of that fashion. In the art of the garden no style is ever lost, no style for ever out of date.

The French practised Renaissance gardening in their own way, and superlatively, the style finding expression through the genius of Le Nôtre and other artists. The greatest work of French garden art is Versailles. But gardens more pleasing, at least to my taste, if less impressive, are to be found around some of the châteaux of the Loire country and elsewhere. But the style is Italianate. It is true that gallicised modifications of that style reached England and Ireland; but it does not seem to me that French gardening need be considered as one of the elements of Irish gardening despite the layout of, for example, Fota and Powerscourt; at most, gallicised Italianate. There were other, minor, modifications and some of them not so minor at that: for example, the influence of the Dutch was briefly important in late Jacobean gardening. But the next major new school in European garden designing was English and must be considered as the fourth element of the Irish garden: this is the landscape garden of the eighteenth and nineteenth centuries.

Under the influence of Italian and Italianate French landscape painting, the English did something entirely new and very remarkable in the art of the garden: they created ideal landscapes not in paint on canvas as the French *paysagistes* were doing, but in the elements of real landscape, earth, water, trees and buildings. The greatest artist, in that he created the principal work of art in this field, was an amateur, the banker Hoare of Stourhead whose masterpiece remains, not quite unchanged indeed, but more or less as he made it. Many professional artists worked in the same manner, the most industrious being Lancelot "Capability" Brown, the most sensitive and original, Humphrey Repton. Their work affected Irish gardens both directly and indirectly. And like the styles already discussed it is still to be seen in existing Irish gardens, and it has been important in the creation of large Irish gardens ever since the early nineteenth century.

The next great change, the next major garden art style to become an element of the Irish garden, was one peculiarly suitable for Ireland. It was favoured by the Irish climate and by Irish soils so that gardens made in this new style reached a level of excellence rather rarely achieved elsewhere. This is the style again originally English which—at the risk of confusion with a medieval Italian style often called by the same name—I called, in my *The English Garden,* the paradise garden.

In that book I sought to show that when the formal, anglicised Italian and French garden art styles of the seventeenth century, modified by such great gardeners as Loudon to produce

Azaleas at Rowallane in May. The wild garden planting of this great garden, now managed by the National Trust, is remarkable for the number and quality of its rhododendron species, including notably the azalea series. The garden has given its name to more than one outstandingly fine garden plant, for example, *Hypericum* x 'Rowallane'.

an English Italianate style, were used by nineteenth-century gardeners in a combination with the eighteenth-century landscape styles, something new emerged. This new combination of formal and landscape gardening was enriched and changed again, late in the nineteenth and early in the twentieth centuries, by a lavish new material, the exotic but more or less hardy plants in huge numbers of species introduced by the plant collectors working in Asia, the Americas, and Australasia.

By the last decades of the nineteenth century there had come into existence in England a new kind of garden, a new school of the gardening art, for which there was no name and to which no particular name was ever given. The new gardens, like the eighteenth-century landscape gardens, were copied all over the civilized world. In *The English Garden*, as I have said, I called them paradise gardens, borrowing from the sixteenth-century use of the word paradise in this context; the use, for instance, with which Parkinson made punning play in the title of his great horticultural book *Paradisus in sole*.

There are many examples of the art of paradise gardening in England: some outstandingly good ones are, in three different styles—Nymans in Sussex, creation of the gifted Messel family and now cared for by the Earl and Countess of Rosse and the National Trust; the Savill gardens in Windsor Great Park created by Sir Eric Savill, Hidcote Barton Manor garden, creation of that great artist Lawrence Johnston and, again, maintained by the National Trust; and Dartington Hall gardens in South Devon, creation of Mr and Mrs Leonard Elmhirst, Miss Beatrix Farrand, and Mr Percy Cane, the newest, and one of the most beautiful of the paradise gardens, in layout and design perhaps the best of all. It is with gardens of this kind, which in Ireland and in one very important respect reached a zenith of perfection, that we shall be concerned in this book.

It is not without some diffidence that I am obliged to point out that it was under English influence that Ireland's paradise gardens, like those of Italy, Portugal, and United States and other countries, were created. For the English invented the style—as they invented one of the major styles which fore-ran it, that of the landscape garden. Attempts have been made to deny this and to show that the eighteenth and early nineteenth-century English landscape gardens which fore-ran the late nineteenth and early twentieth-century paradise gardens, had their origin in Chinese landscape gardening.

There are, perhaps, a few Irishmen still left who would prefer to owe their country's gardening style to ancient China than to England; I apologise to them for showing, I think successfully, in the book already referred to, that several of the earliest, and above all the greatest, masterpieces of the landscape art were in being before any influence from China can have been at work. It is true that such great works of art as Stourhead and Sheffield Park are reminiscent of the great Chinese landscape gardens in so far as we know what these were like: but the likeness is attributable to a similarity of taste, a particular

The Neptune in the lake at Powerscourt near Dublin.

approach to nature, secular and poetical and yet very practical, of the Chinese and the English mandarin classes. Irish paradise gardens owe nothing but plants to ancient Chinese gardening.

It will be as well here to re-define what I mean by a paradise garden. There are various expressions of the style, and not all the elements of the ideal garden are present in all examples; I will take a case in which, however, this is so: the elements are those we have been discussing and the first element is therefore the Italian garden. The Renaissance garden of Italy was a sort of *al fresco* drawing-room, a seemly and pleasantly furnished place in which to spend leisure. The materials of its composition were buildings and such masonry structure as walls, arches and balustraded stairways; evergreens, more or less restrained in their growth, often clipped into geometrical but not into fancy shapes; trees; and some statuary. These were composed by art into a unity. The next element is the landscape garden of the eighteenth century of which Stourhead is the most perfect example. The maker of such a garden used a whole piece of country, hills, rivers, lakes, trees as his materials, and he worked in precisely the spirit of such landscape painters as Claude and Poussin, creating, in natural materials instead of paint and in full size instead of miniature, an ideal landscape to replace the aesthetically less pleasing real one. In the nineteenth century gardens were made in which both these styles were respected, often in reaction

The Bay of Glengariff from one of Harold Peto's Italianate pavilions in Ilnacullin.

against the mere "riot-of-colour" gardens which new technical advances had made all too possible.

In the late nineteenth and early twentieth centuries English gardeners, under the influence chiefly of an Irishman, one of the greatest figures in the history of gardening, William Robinson, reacted against all the more or less formal styles, including stylised landscape gardening, in favour of a style which became known as Wild, or Woodland, gardening. The idea was to create absolutely "natural" open woodland scenes into which were planted, "after nature", large numbers of both native and exotic plants. There must be no effort to arrange the plant material after any school of art, nature only must be copied, the only departure from her sweet disorder being that plant species not ordinarily found growing together could be used.

Robinson was born in Ireland in 1838 of poor and obscure parents, and nothing is known about his boyhood. He started as gardener's boy on the outdoor staff of a clerical baronet, and at the age of twenty-one he was head gardener. The story of how he came to leave this job is a very odd one. Geoffrey Taylor, in his *Some Nineteenth Century Gardeners* says that one night in the bitter winter of 1861 Robinson opened all the lights of his employers' hothouses, drew the boiler fires, and bolted for Dublin. Why he did this extraordinary thing, which resulted in the loss of hundreds of valuable exotic plants, is not known, but it can only have been in revenge for some wrong or slight, and it demonstrated the passionate temper which was to be a trial and tribulation to his associates during much of his life. The curious thing is that David Moore, director of the Botanic Gardens at Glasnevin, Dublin, did not hesitate to give Robinson a letter of introduction and recommendation to Marnock, then curator of the Botanic Gardens in Regent's Park, London. He may, of course, not have known about Robinson's behaviour to his late employer; or he may have known and sympathised with the reason for it. Marnock gave the young Irishman a job in the herbaceous section of the botanic gardens: the plants in this section were all natives, and one of Robinson's jobs was to collect specimens. In the course of this work he conceived a passion for native British plants and for the simple cottage gardens of the villages.

> "Out of this passion arose his vision: he saw a garden in which nature, so mild and lovely in England, should not be coerced and deformed but aided and abetted to do her best by the planting of exotics not merely in but, as it were *into*, the native scene."
>
> (E. Hyams, *The English Garden*)

It is not necessary here to go into the rest of Robinson's remarkable career: he went from success to success, not only as a gardener and botanist but as a publisher of horticultural journals and as the maker of the great garden of Gravetye, his home in the latter part of his life. His greatest fault was impatience: some of his schemes, involving the moving of many fully grown trees or the simultaneous planting of tens of thousands of bulbs, were costly failures. But it is pleasantly appropriate that the man who created the style of gardening most suitable for and most successful in Ireland should have been an Irishman. He was one of those brilliant creative men whose radiant vitality and conviction change the ways of their comtemporaries, and for some time, under the influence of his driving energy, Wild Gardens became *de rigueur*. Robinson was not, however, as fanatical and as incapable of considering that he might be mistaken as has often been claimed: for example he worked with and was strongly influenced by Gertrude Jekyll and he modified his own ideas because he respected hers. And it was under her influence that some beginning of a reaction against the Wild Garden set in.

It was, then, out of a mixture of Italianate formal gardening, English landscape gardening, and Robinsonian Wild Gardening that the nineteenth/twentieth-century paradise garden was created: and this style was brought to perfection in the very favourable conditions of Ireland, both north and south.

If I called such gardens "paradise" gardens it was because it seemed to me that, consciously or otherwise, the artists — for they were and are artists — who made them were

Mount Stewart. Heraldic statuary against the *Cupressus macrocarpa* arcades.

giving expression to the feeling for pre-Fall-of-Man innocence evoked by the English language version of Genesis. But that is by no means the only comparison which could be made: that feeling for the exotic and romantic, for a colourful jungle tamed by art as formerly paradise was tamed by innocence, for country much richer in the colours and forms of plants than anything afforded by temperate-zone nature in north-west Europe, might also be a by-product of English and Irish contact with the tropics in the course of exploration and imperial adventures.

The makers of paradise gardens were making a possible world, a world in which the most beautiful and interesting plant species, naturally scattered all over the world, were brought together into one place and used as elements of a composition richer than any natural countryside could show, a composition in which plants from the Himalayas grew cheek by jowl with those of the Andes, in which the plant beauties of Australasia supplemented those of China and North America. But, and this is important, the best of these gardeners were not mere plantsmen, they were not simply collecting plants into amateur botanical gardens of the kind invented by the great civilizations of pre-Conquest Mexico and Peru. The materials were new and rich; the traditions of the art of gardening were still respected in the use of it. The paradise gardeners were not scientists but, I repeat, artists.

If, in their climate, relatively so mild for the high latitude of their country, and in their soil, less dominated by limestones than most of Continental Europe, the English had peculiar advantages in the practice of this art, the Irish had the same advantages in even greater measure. A large number of the most beautiful flowering plants in the world come from lower latitudes, but often higher altitudes, than any part of Ireland. But the sea, warmed by the Gulf-stream, ensures for Ireland milder winters and moister summers than any other country of comparable latitude. Trees, shrubs and herbaceous plants from the hilly regions of much more southerly lands find there the mildness and the high rainfall which they need. Ireland is not by, say, Italian standards, a sunny country; but she has enough sunshine to satisfy the needs of plants which come, as the most beautiful do, from lands in which the sky is very often overcast. I know of only one climate in which I would rather grow flowering shrubs, fine trees and herbaceous plants; it is that of the north-west coast of Portugal.

A glance at a good isothermic map of Ireland and Great Britain will show the isotherms of the critical mean minimum January temperature running not east to west but, roughly, north to south: in other words, it is not the north which is colder than the south in this region of the world, but, rather, and with reservations, the east which is colder than the west. More accurately, it is the north-east which is colder than the south-west. With the exception of an inland area, most of Ireland is outside (above) the January mean minimum

Among the exotics flourishing in Irish gardens are tree ferns, *Dicksonia*.

Sunlight striking through foliage reveals the beauty of tree bark.

isotherm 40 degrees F., and much of it above 43 degrees F. Frosts are fewer and less severe than in England with the exception of south-west Cornwall and the Scilly Isles. And this fact has had an important influence on the nature of the plant material used in the making of Irish gardens.

And so, of course, has the nature of the Irish soil. By comparison with other European countries, Ireland has little limestone and a lot of peat; the soils of much of Ireland are acid. Now while it is true that a vast number of very beautiful plants can be grown to perfection in limestone soils, and even in chalk, it is also the case that a great many of the most beautiful cannot. Not only are ericaceous plants, which include rhododendrons, with few exceptions intolerant of lime, but so are many of the finest shrubs and trees and herbaceous genera introduced from South America and Australasia. Such plants flourish in Ireland's peat.

To sum up: the origins of the Irish garden as discussed in this work and illustrated are, in design, the Italianate gardens of the seventeenth century and the landscape gardens of the eighteenth; the spirit and plant material, the romantic paradise gardens of the late nineteenth century and the early twentieth, pioneered by, among others, the Irish-born William Robinson who made the great romantic garden of "Gravetye" in Sussex; in soil, peat; in climate, the softness which distinguishes all the seasons in Ireland. But in gardening as in everything else in Ireland rather more often than elsewhere there are, as we shall see, exceptions.

The formal fountain basins at Castlewellan, Co. Down, are embellished by background planting of copper-leaved shrubs. This garden has one of the finest collections of exotic trees in the world, planted in the park-like style of eighteenth century English landscape gardening.

2

Mount Usher

I consider the garden of Mount Usher Mill to be the most nearly perfect example of the romantic, paradise, Robinsonian garden, revealing hardly a trace of the earlier styles represented in the gardens of Ireland. It is entirely successful in combining plantsmanship in which such gardens excel, with a layout—one cannot properly call it design for the gardens have grown and were never planned as a whole from the start—which idealises to perfection a possible natural world.

Mount Usher is in the village of Ashford in County Wicklow, about thirty miles south of Dublin. The house stands back from, and the garden is laid out along, a reach of the River Vartry. The soil is for the most part sandy gravel with some small areas of clay, and it is acid. The climate of the garden is humid and remarkably mild, surprisingly so, indeed, for in very harsh winters the thermometer does not fall as low there as in the very mild west of Ireland and the garden has rarely suffered more than ten degrees Fahrenheit of frost.

The late Mr E. H. Walpole, one of the half dozen greatest gardeners of our time, has himself given an account of how his family first came to be interested in and then to acquire the property where their great garden was to be created (*Mount Usher, Wicklow*, Mount Usher, 1952). At the time Mount Usher was still a working water-mill.

"My grandfather, Edward Walpole, Senior, was, like most men of his generation, very fond of walking, and he particularly admired the romantic scenery of County Wicklow. He used frequently to go to Hunter's Hotel, Newrathbridge, a comfortable centre for his rambles. In the course of his visits and excursions he encountered Sam Sutton of Mount Usher Mill and became very friendly with him. After a time the miller suggested that instead of staying at the hotel my grandfather should stay at the mill, a suggestion that was adopted. . . . In 1868, when Sam Sutton's lease of the Mill expired, a new lease . . . was taken out by Edward Walpole; the area stated in the lease being one acre and eleven perches only. . . ."

Subsequently—in 1875—Edward Walpole, who was then 77 years old, transferred his interest in the property to his sons Thomas, George and Edward. If, as a result, George and Edward were to become gardeners, Thomas was able to find expression for a taste for civil engineering and architectural design; it was he who altered the mill weir and who designed the first of the pretty little suspension bridges which at various points connect the two parts of the garden which are on opposite sides of the Vartry.

I suppose that the actual beginning of the gardens was the substitution, by Edward Walpole, of flowers for potatoes in the plot of land before the house. Edward also planted some trees, notably a sequoia, and a tsuga by the house which had to be felled half a century later because it had become a danger to the house. And whatever he planted flourished, partly because the conditions were so very good, and partly also because he was a man who gave proper care to whatever he undertook. In the 1870s the ultimate enlargement of the garden was envisaged when new plots of land were bought on the same side of the river as the house itself.

Now here is what Edward's grandson wrote in his own account of the gardens about the principal influence under which Mount Usher gardens were created:

"Early in the eighties there was a new movement in British and Irish gardening. It was at this period that William Robinson—the author of *The English Flower Garden,* and who may justly be called the father of modern English gardening—started his campaign against the formal fashions that had long been dominant, and pleaded that trees and shrubs should be allowed to grow more or less naturally. George and Edward Walpole were his disciples and introduced his methods into Mount Usher. The success that attended their efforts is apparent, and in this way my father and uncle did a great deal to encourage horticultural tastes and interest in Ireland."

Late in the eighties still further enlargement of the gardens became desirable and land was acquired on the other, the south-west, side of the river, for the first time. Thomas Walpole built his first suspension bridge. More land was bought in 1891 and in 1899, by which time the gardens, or land for them as they were extended, exceeded four acres. Most of this land was planted with trees and shrubs, and by 1916 the four acres had, by means of various purchases and leases, grown to ten. By then George and Thomas Walpole

Mount Usher. The central axis of this great paradise garden is the river with its series of waterfalls.

had died, and Edward Walpole, junior, was sole owner of the property. He died, however, in 1917, and his interest in Mount Usher, in both senses of the word fell to the late Mr E. H. Walpole.

Until 1927 the Walpole family were leaseholders of Mount Usher, but in that year a chance occurred and was taken to acquire the freehold together with that of an adjoining three acres. Yet another two acres were purchased on the west side of the river, bringing the whole property up to fifteen acres, and a final land acquisition in 1946 brought the gardens to their present shape and extent. Meanwhile more bridges had been built, so had a house for the head gardener; and the house itself had been rebuilt. And by this time planting had been going on continuously for fifty years.

Mount Usher's first head gardener was Charles Fox: his service was long, for he was appointed in 1897 and he worked in the gardens without a break until 1942. His assistant Michael Giffney succeeded him. For the most part the record of the gardens during Fox's time was one of steady and gratifying progress but there were, of course, some set-backs, notably in 1931 when the Vartry overflowed its banks and there was serious flooding; and in the winter of 1939/40 when twenty-six degrees of frost killed a considerable number of exotics which had flourished for many years.

PLANTING

The Walpoles, as they were and are the first to acknowledge, were very fortunate, as gardeners, in the friendship and help of Sir Frederick W. Moore, sometime Director of the then Royal and now National, Botanic Gardens, Glasnevin. I am able to draw for an account of his connection with Mount Usher on his own Recollections of the gardens, written in 1928 and published in Mr E. H. Walpole's *Mount Usher* in 1952. Sir Frederick first went to Mount Usher in 1885. He met the three Walpole brothers; and he saw at once that the situation of the gardens was an exceptionally favourable one in the matter of soil, water and climate. He realised that any plant which could be grown in the open anywhere in the British Isles would do well at Mount Usher, and also that George and Edward Walpole had not fully grasped the possibilities of their garden, if only because only a professional botanist could possibly have a sufficiently wide knowledge of plants. He decided to keep them supplied with the names of new exotics to try, and to help them to plant material much of which would be rare and hard to obtain in Ireland or Britain. It must be said, however, that considering the Walpoles were linen drapers, not botanists, they were already doing pretty well, for Sir Frederick himself says:

"At that date many plants now common were scarce and difficult to obtain, but a considerable number of these rarer plants were already at Mount Usher. I have

Mount Usher. The most beautiful plants from every part of the world are combined to form an integral work of art.

vivid recollections of the impression made by certain plants on that memorable day. A splendid plant of a very vigorous form of *Rosa brunonia*, in full flower, covered the roof of an outhouse and hung down into the yard on the other side, scenting the air all round. *Buddleia colvillei* was in flower on the same building, and on the dwelling house *Mandevilla suaveolens* was in full flower. On another wall *Berberidopsis corallina* and *Schizophragma hydrangeoides* flowered side by side, while great bushes of *Abutilon vitifolium* flowered in the open near them. *Eugenia apiculata* and *Crinodendron hookerianum*, as they were then called, were in flower, both fair-sized plants, also the little known *Rosa hemisphaerica*. Then and now one of the striking features of Mount Usher were the stately groups of *Cordyline australis* which gave a peculiarly tropical look to their surroundings quite in keeping with the nature of the place. Turn which way one might one found interesting and remarkable plants; good specimens of *Pittosporums, Escallonia philippiana, E. pterocladon, E. montevidensis, Sophora tetraptera, Olearia forsteri, O. traversi, Parrotia, Azara, Cunninghamia sinensis, Abelia trifolora* and *Stauntonia latifolia* clambered high up into the lime-trees. The Walpoles highly prized a fine form of *Acer japonicum* with upright habit, the bark of which turned in autumn and winter to a good red colour, and during the summer to pink and pale orange: this was christened 'The Coral Bark Maple'. It still flourishes and maintains its peculiarities."

All this had been accomplished by 1885. The two gardener Walpoles worked in the gardens themselves almost every weekend for nine months of every year. The garden as we now see it is almost four times as large as it was then. The energy, the money and the zeal which were applied to this grand work are all made very clear by another paragraph of Sir Frederick Moore's Recollections:

"It became difficult to find space for newcomers, and the plants already there began to crowd each other, therefore more land was taken, first on one side of the river, then on the other. Bridges were constructed to replace stepping-stones, and a gradual transference of the plants from the older to the newer grounds was carried out. Certain genera such as *Rhododendron, Azalea, Eucalyptus, Magnolia, Acacia,* etc., which were not well represented were taken in hand and brought up to date. Edward's energy was given full play, and nurseries in Great Britain, France, Italy and Germany were ransacked for desired plants. Consignments of seed came from New Zealand and Australia, also a large importation of plants from Japan, which proved to be a successful venture."

And, again:

Mount Usher. *Pinus montezumae*, loveliest of its genus, a native of Mexico, is one of the great ornaments of this garden.

"Climbers and trailing plants were planted to clothe the stems of trees; many excellent effects have been obtained. Long slender branches of *Solanum crispum* hanging downwards covered with blue flowers are wonderfully effective. Lapagerias, both red and white, grow freely, flower freely, and fruit, producing fertile seed. *Schizandra rubriflora* against an old ash-tree is very striking when the sun shines on its flowers, and equally good effects are obtained from other plants.

"One of the most effective achievements is the fernery. A small stream runs between deep banks with tall, shade-giving trees on either side. There is not sufficient space to make a narrow path, so access is obtained by means of planks on iron supports running down the middle of the stream, a few inches above the water. Both banks are covered with ferns, and such tender species as *Trichomanes radicans, T. reniforme, Hymenophyllum demissum, Todea pellucida, T. superba woodwardia radicans* have flourished for years."

By 1928, when Sir Frederick wrote his Recollections, the garden had, as we have seen, grown not only in extent but in riches. For the benefit of those plantsmen who would find it interesting, a very long list of the plants chosen as the most interesting growing at Mount Usher at that time was made by Mr J. W. Besant, Curator of the Botanic Gardens, Glasnevin, until 1945. The list appears in Mr E. H. Walpole's *Mount Usher, Wicklow*, published at Mount Usher in 1952.

From the horticultural historical point of view, we are fortunate in having a series of accounts of the gardens, made by competent people at various points in their history: thus, those of Sir Frederick Moore and of Mr Besant, already referred to; thus, too, those of Mr G. C. Taylor, in 1936, and Mr Lanning Roper in 1951.

One thing which Mr Taylor makes clear is that in 1936 when the gardens were getting on for seventy years old, Robinsonian principles were still paramount. Having given us a long list of the names of the rarer exotics which he had seen in the gardens, he wrote:

"These newcomers were all skilfully associated with the native trees and the varied wild growths about the place and, by picturesque grouping and the absence of anything like striving after purely artificial effects, or apparent botanic system or scientific collection in their choice and placing, many of these, now trees in their proportions, play their part in a scheme where nature still dominates and artifice is her handmaid faithfully falling into her ways. Since those early days planting has gone on almost uninterruptedly until the present time, as choice became wider and more varied with the vast influx of new plants, most of which are particularly well adapted to the conditions of soil and climate offered by Mount Usher." (*Country Life*, July 4, 1936.)

Mount Usher. The garden is long and narrow, extending along both banks of the river, which thus provides its principal axis. A rich alluvial soil, ample rainfall, high sunshine hours and mild winters favour the exotic plants which make this one of the grandest romantic gardens in the world.

Mount Usher. One of the riverside walks showing the exquisitely planted banks.

The fashion in which Robinsonian gardening was practised had also clearly made an impression on this observer:

"The presence of the River Vartry, which runs through the garden and is joined lower down by a small stream entering from the north side, contributes not a little to the many natural beauties of the place and has provided the owners with many opportunities for the planting of a host of waterside and moisture-loving plants, of which they have not been slow to take advantage. Bridges cross the river at intervals and afford the visitor the most attractive vistas along the quietly furnished banks, where colonies of many *Primula* species like *japonica, pulverulenta, bulleyana helodoxa, sikkimensis,* and *florindae;* mimulus, globe flowers, and irises like *laevigata* and *sibirica*, revel in the moist soil and semi-shade. All these, too, find a place by the margins of the water-lily pond, where they have the companionship of various spiraeas and astilbes and the handsome *Lysichitum americanum* whose distinguished yellow spathes are succeeded by large and grand leaves for which

Exotic conifers as a foil for *Eucryphia* x 'Mount Usher'.

alone the plant is worth growing. Near the pond in the shade of tall alders which of yore formed a grove, many choice trees, shrubs and hardy plants have been skilfully grouped together, and among the most noteworthy are *Acacia dealbata*, which has assumed the stature of a tree; magnificent specimens of *Tricuspidaria lanceolata*, which glow with their crimson lanterns in June; *Leptospermum chapmanni*, smothered in deep pink blossoms; *Euonymus bungeanus*, several magnolias including a fine specimen of *M. wilsoni; Cinnamonum camphora* some twenty-five feet high; *Lomatia ferruginea;* and the late summer-flowering *Hoheria lanceolata*. Many species of hybrid rhododendrons are also represented here, and flanking one of the paths under the alders is a fine planting of the distinguished *Viburnum tomentosum mariesii*, with a ground carpet of funkias and ferns, providing the most charming picture in early June, the effect of which is enhanced by various climbers like *Lapageria rosea. Solanum crispum* and *Schizandra rubriflora*, which luxuriate on the stems and branches of the trees, giving an almost subtropical look to the woodland. Elsewhere are colonies of the handsome New Zealand *Myosotidium nobile*, which seems to have found exactly the right conditions in the half shade and damp soil, judging by its luscious appearance and its unforgettable display of bright blue flowers; and in among the shrubs are groups of various lilies, meconopsis, primulas, and herbaceous things, which revel in the situation and afford fine patches of colour all through late spring and summer.

Mount Usher. Close planting of the waterside is a feature in this garden.

"Across the river a series of rocky beds raised above the water level accommodate many rock and alpine treasures; and beyond, a path leads to the nurseries, concealed from sight by a high brick wall, with several short walls built at right angles to the main wall, thus providing a series of alcoves enclosed on three sides, which provide a comfortable home, for many tall shrubs like *Malva capensis*, *M. maritima, Dendromecon rigidum, Fremontia californica, Schizandra sphaenanthera, Acacia baileyana*, various grevilleas, and *Callistemon salignus*. On a bank near by, Farrer's threepenny-bit rose has spread itself and keeps company in June with the lovely *Geranium anemonaefolium*. Continuing along the path, a small summer-house is reached which affords a charming view of the house across an expanse of lawn flanked by Japanese maples, and the river, whose margins are lined with mimulus and primulus." (*Ibid.*)

Mr Taylor seems to have been the first articulate visitor at Mount Usher to be as much struck as I was myself when I first went there more than twenty years later, by the great beauty and distinction of the eucalyptus, and especially of the white-stemmed specimens of *E. viminalis* trees at least 150 feet tall; and of the magnificent conifer *Pinus montezumae*, surely the most beautiful species of its genus and especially so in the very glaucous Mount Usher form.

Mr Lanning Roper, writing an account of the garden in 1951, was perhaps the first visitor to apply the eye—and criticism—of a talented garden designer to Mount Usher, not allowing himself to be entirely swept away by the plants and plantsmanship displayed:

"The design of the garden has been influenced in large measure by the narrowness of the site. The property follows the river and unfortunately lacks breadth. It has been added to from time to time. . . . As a result there are some excellent vistas along the river and roughly parallel to it, but it is difficult to view the plantings from other vantage points. Recent additions have been made with an eye to correcting this. By skilful planting and opening up, the very most is being made of an unusually difficult problem.

"By good fortune some of the earliest plantings included sequoias, tsugas, and other large trees which have become fine specimens today and provide the basic frame for the garden. A few years is all the time needed for the new additions to take on an established look, so skilfully is the planting done and so favourable is the climate. The rate of growth is a very sobering revelation to those of us who garden in less clement areas, and it makes possible the rapid establishment of new schemes."

Eucryphia x 'Mount Usher' flowers in September.

Mr Roper then goes on to describe some of the more interesting plants and he draws a conclusion which is true of Mount Usher as of all the best romantic or "paradise" gardens:

"It is the mixture of the exotic with the natural freshness and greenness that makes the gardens of the British Isles so far more satisfying than those of the Mediterranean or the tropics.

"At Mount Usher this effect has to a certain extent been an unconscious achievement. Plants are placed on the basis of their requirements of soil, shade, moisture, etc. Suitability to conditions of good growth and protection, rather than purely aesthetic consideration, which too often dictates in these matters, is of paramount importance. This has resulted in unusual combinations of material. Secondly, there has been no attempt to cultivate the tender and the rare exclusively. These may become too much the objective, and then the lovely native things and the old favourites are excluded. Not so the garden at Mount Usher. The Walpoles have always been extremely catholic in their tastes, liking all genera and trying any noteworthy newcomer."*

A number of visitors to this great garden have published accounts of it; there is one of the best to which the reader may like to refer, by Mr R. C. Jenkinson, in the *Journal* of the Royal Horticultural Society. Mr Jenkinson wrote his account in the year 1958 and it is now useful, in the main, as a means of judging the progress of the garden, the persistence and prosperity of certain plants, and disappearance of others. He does not, of course, supply a complete plant list, and as far as I know no *Hortus* of the garden has ever been attempted; but he does note, for example, that certain tender species of trees and shrubs, e.g. *Agathis australis* and *Tecophilaea cyanocrocus*, and certain others tender enough to have been damaged by the severe frosts of 1956, e.g. *Olearea hectori*, were still flourishing.

Furthermore, such past accounts of Mount Usher serve to reveal its status as one of the gardens in which plantsmanship has been pioneered, as it were. For example, writing of the long narrow bank, path, border and wall between the Vartry and one of the roads through Ashford, which forms one extreme of the garden and which was relatively newly planted when he was there—the 'Riviera'—Mr Jenkinson picks out the callistemons for special notice. By the time I saw them in flower at Mount Usher, some years later, I was fairly used to seeing them in south-western gardens, was growing them myself in Devonshire and knew them as by no means as uncommon as they had been. Many such Australasian plants, tried at Mount Usher almost as early as at Nymans and much less liable to frost damage there, have since been shown to be less tender than was at first supposed, not only callistemons but one or two grevilleas, some melaleucas and, of course, several species of

*Mr Lanning Roper's study of this garden appeared in Mr E. H. Walpole's *Mount Usher* already quoted.

A discreet use of more or less hardy palms, e.g. *Trachycarpus*, enhances the romantic exoticism of Mount Usher.

the southern hemisphere beeches, *Nothofagus*. Nor is this true only of Australasians: *Cistus pahlinhai*, cited by Mr Jenkinson in his R.H.S. *Journal* account as "fairly new" has become relatively common in great gardens; and the use of *Lapageria rosea* out of doors, noted as unusual ten years ago, is now much less so.

My own first visit to Mount Usher was made in autumn, and although the garden should be visited at all seasons, and especially in May, one of its most striking successes can be seen properly in September and October. As a rule the eucryphias for which it is very remarkable will still be in bloom, especially the enormous *E. cordifolia* groups. The Chilean species, and their hybrid of which more below, have reached a size and girth at Mount Usher which can be equalled in very few gardens, and the flowering of the *E. cordifolia*, in groups which must be over thirty feet tall and as much through, is something to be seen. The New Zealand and Australian species are also represented, of course, and above all the hybrid *E. cordifolia* x *E. gluttinosa* which should, I suppose, be called either *E.* x 'Mount Usher' or *E.* x *mountusherensis*, is very fine. This originally appeared as a chance seedling and would no doubt be much better known and more widely planted than it is had not precisely the same chance cross occured at Nymans first, so that it is *E.* x 'Nymans' which is in general cultivation and not the nearly identical *E.* x 'Mount Usher'. At the same season as the eucryphias and for a week or two later the success of the remarkable plantings for autumn colour can be seen and admired. Why is it that not only this Irish garden, but several others, are so much better for autumn colour than any English garden known to me? In the theory most generally accepted — that good autumn colour depends on dry summers followed by a sudden frost — Irish gardens should be less successful in this respect than English gardens. At Mount Usher the spectacular effects are obtained by plantings of the deciduous azaleas, among the best plants for this purpose; of *Enkianthus campanulatus*, *E. cernuus*, *E. perulatus* and perhaps other species of this genus; of the Japanese *Disanthus cerdifolius*, in my own experience the most vivid of all the species which turn scarlet, crimson or purple in autumn; of *Acer* — Mr Jenkinson picked out 'Osakazuki' as the most brilliant during his own visit; and, for lighter shades, Tulip and Maidenhair trees, the newcomer Dawn Redwood and its relative the Swamp Cypress *Taxodium distichum*. The American and Chinese cornels, too, are remarkable for their autumn colour.

In his account of Mount Usher, and in other published accounts of this garden, Mr Jenkinson gives much attention to the rare and exotic plants there, but I am anxious not to present this garden in terms of a plant list. I must make some attempt to give my own general impression of this garden, having leaned so heavily on that of other and more qualified authors. No more, then, about the plants themselves: what counts with me is the effect of the whole, an effect which makes me place this garden first among all the basically "Robinsonian" gardens known to me. There are particular impressions of parts which,

No garden in Europe exceeds Mount Usher in the variety and diversity of foliage. The trees and flowering shrubs of South America, Australia, New Zealand, West China, North Africa and all Europe flourish like natives in a perfectly integrated composition.

One of the numerous river vistas at Mount Usher, embellished by banks of azaleas.

combined, make up the general impression of the whole: the sunshine on the gently waving silver-blue-green foliage of the great Montezuma pine; the towering white stems of gum trees against a clear blue sky and their elegantly pendent sage-green leaves, so sharp and shapely against that same background. Bees loud and busy in the eucryphia flowers; the scarlets and golds of the enkianthus which made so strong an impression on Mr Jenkinson; the vistas, half a dozen different ones, down the Vartry and its cunningly gardened banks, evoking boyhood dreams and stories of exploring in remote and alien places.

And there it is, my real point about this garden, its astonishing evocative power, the evocative power of a perfectly successful work of romantic art. What the Walpoles have done here is to create a possible world, just as the romantic novelist or painter does, bringing together elements of natural beauty from all over the world into one place, and using imagination to form them into a composition. Nature has scattered her plant masterpieces all over the world; Mount Usher places them, in a scene which is nevertheless perfectly "natural", side by side with an art which makes the ideal seem to be a sample of the real.

41

3

Annes Grove

If Mount Usher stands to perfection for the styles and tradition of Robinsonian gardening, for the art of the "paradise" garden in Ireland, then the two Annesley gardens, Annes Grove in the south and Castlewellan in the north, but particularly Annes Grove, seem to me to stand for the most perfect combination of "paradise" woodland gardening with a touch of the more formal styles mentioned in Chapter 1. These two gardens achieve this in different ways and according to different periods in the history of the art. The touch of the formal at Castlewellan is in the grand manner which derives from eighteenth, ultimately seventeenth century styles. At Annes Grove it is derived from the nineteenth century, from the cult of the flower-garden and of the herbaceous border. I think that one could, if it served any purpose, trace at Annes Grove the influence of three great gardener-artists: that of Loudon, remotely; that of William Robinson, principally; and that of Gertrude Jekyll, for example, in the cottagey-look of the enclosed parts of the garden.

Annes Grove is near the small town of Castletownroche in County Cork, a county very favourable to almost all kinds of gardening. The mean January minimum temperature is 44 degrees F., the rainfall ample, the soil deep and rich, for the most part on the acid side of neutral but with some lime in places. The property which is the site of the house and garden was anciently known as Ballyhimock, The Place of the Rock. As a gentleman's residence it dates from the seventeenth century. The Grove family, who settled in Ireland from England in 1605, later acquired this property. Still later it came into the Annesley family by the marriage of an Annesley to a Grove heiress. The Annesleys are of very much more ancient Irishry than the Groves: they trace their descent from a knight, presumably Norman, Anneslei by name, who settled in Ireland late in the eleventh century.

The garden as we have it now, however, is the creation of Mr Richard Grove Annesley*, the present owner, and his late wife, working upon beginnings made by Mr Annesley's

*Since this was written Mr Annesley has died.

The mild climate of County Cork makes Annes Grove one of the most flourishing collections of exotic plants in Europe.

father. It has, therefore, been made within one man's lifetime; even many of the immense trees, which look some centuries old, were in fact planted by Mr Annesley as a young man perhaps half a century ago. What Mr Lanning Roper wrote of Mount Usher, I can write of Annes Grove, that it is a sobering thought to those of us who garden in less favourable conditions, to see the rate and health of growth in all kinds of plants in the wonderfully soft climate of Cork and under the skilful care of such a gardener as Mr Annesley.

From the point of view of its extraordinary wealth and range of plant material, Annes Grove benefited from Mr Annesley's participation as a shareholder in several of the plant-hunting expeditions of the first half of the twentieth century, and notably in those of the late Frank Kingdon-Ward. A number of the fine rhododendrons of this garden, which is so rich in that genus, still bear no names but only the Kingdon-Ward collection numbers. But it should be said at once that Mr Annesley is no mere plantsman, that I have watched him at work supervising, at more than eighty years of age incidentally, the replanting of his garden, and recognized the skill of a true designer of gardens; and that his eye for combinations of plants, for vistas, and even for garden geometry in the appropriate places, is excellent.

The gardens can be divided into roughly five areas: the sweep or drive, and yards, in the immediate neighbourhood of the house, including the terrace behind the house; the Walled Garden; the Water Garden, the bank dominating the water garden; and the Woodland or Wild Garden. The Woodland Garden is perhaps the most important part; it is at once one of the finest collections of flowering trees and shrubs in these islands; and one of the most successfully planned plantings of exotics into native woodland, on the Robinsonian plan, that I know. The woodland is extensive and the shape and fall of the land are full of interest: at one moment you are looking steeply down into a glen of incredibly romantic opulence, dominated by fine broad-leaved trees and exotic conifers, but vivid with the flowers of scores of Chinese and Himalayan rhododendrons. At the next, you are looking at a slope dominated by a magnificent specimen of one of the many embothriums, or, again, staring along a vista of soft colour overhung by many greens, where the long golden racemes of *Laburnum vossii* hang down across a walk or drive. A splendid specimen of the silver-leaved *Cornus contraversa* halts you for a moment, but you are soon drawn on to identify the great gold and white lily-like flowers of some quite unfamiliar rhododendron, or to inspect more closely, crossing an emerald sward, the waxy apricot or crimson bells of a whole coppice of rhododendrons of the *cinnabarinum* series.

The Chilean genera of flowering trees and shrubs are very much at home in Annes Grove's woods: in June the crinodendrons are gorgeously decorated with their rose-pink lanterns. In early autumn the South American eucryphias, immense specimens only to be matched at Mount Usher, are covered with their white cup flowers, and their golden centres

Eucryphia cordifolia attains a stature of forty feet in many Irish gardens.

are alive with bees which are so fond of this genus that in both Chile and New Zealand it is an important honey plant. But Australasian plants do equally well — the New Zealand and Australian eucryphias in late summer, at other seasons the oleareas, including the lovely *Olearea semidendata,* with its fine daisies of deep mauve disc florets and pale mauve or white ray florets; this daisy bush is surpassed among the oleareas only by the allied *O. chatamica* which would, no doubt, be just as flourishing there.

As in all the gardens of County Cork, exotic and native plants reach a great size very quickly and have an excellence, a distinction of form and bearing which are, perhaps, no more than signs of robust health. It is not only a matter of mild, soft air, ample rainfall, and deep, usually acid and often alluvial soil — though parts of Annes Grove have a surprisingly high *p*H for so successful a rhododendron garden. It is just as much a matter of good gardening, cultivation, mulching, the cutting out of dead wood, and all such persistent care.

In autumn the gardens, and especially parts of the woodland and more parklike planting near the house, are remarkable for the flowering of innumerable hoherias, many of them self-sown seedlings, hybrids between the species originally planted; and for autumn colour. The colour — gold, crimson, scarlet and purple — has, of course, been planned for. The outstanding plants in this flaming spectacle are some North American cornus species which, even in late August, are already a rich claret-red; and superlatively, and surely the best of all small trees for autumn colour, *Disanthus cercidifolius* which, even in Devonshire, invariably gives a fiery display. I say "even in Devonshire" in order to introduce a generality on this subject of autumn colour in the Irish garden. Why — and I have seen it in the east at Mount Usher, in the south at Annes Grove, and at Mount Congreve, in the far west at Illnacullin, and in the north at Castlewellan — is this colour so much finer and so much more reliable than in England? When I was in New England to see the autumn colour there, I was told that it depends on summer dryness followed, in autumn, by a sudden sharp frost. But the Irish gardens are exceptionally moist in both soil and air — the climate is the very antithesis of New England's — and as for frost, there rarely is any until January and often none at all. Yet the colouring of the leaves of such genera as *Cornus, Enkianthus, Disanthus,* and *Acer* is far richer than in England's West Country and is, moreover, an annual, not an occasional, event.

Annes Grove's water-garden is dominated by and can be viewed from a great bank richly planted, traversed by many zig-zag paths, and rising steeply from the river level to the much higher house level. It is planted with a wide range of shrubs, herbaceous perennials, bulb plants, alpines. Lower down flourish great colonies of moisture-loving primula — *japonica, florindae,* and many less common, all of them naturalised. Mecanopses do well in this garden as one would expect, the sky-blue *betonicfolia,* the even more beautiful

The ample rainfall of Southern Ireland suits the great primitive giant-leaved rhododendrons of the *grande* series.

electric-blue *grandis* in such forms as 'Blantyre' and, the best, 'Prain'; the creamy yellow or claret red flowered *regia* is there, too, with its great rosettes of hairy, silver leaves.

The basin of the water garden is a quite impressive and very pretty tributary of the river Blackwater, flowing tranquilly through its own little valley. The far bank of this stream is completely curtained, as it were, with a magnificent arundinaria, a plumed bamboo which makes an admirable and rather exotic backcloth for the whole scene. This half-wild, half-planted valley offers a whole series of completely satisfying *coups d'oeil*, both from above, from the many points-of-view at the house level, and from the terrace, a sort of elongated belvedere, just below that level; and, as vistas, from the level of the stream itself. Down there, at the water level, one can follow a network of winding and criss-crossing paths among rocks, borders and water, among primulas, mecanopses and irises, rogersias, gunnera and heaven knows how many exotic, water-loving species, many of which seem to be more or less naturalised. Waterlilies flourish in backwaters, and the great swamp cypress, *Taxodium distichum*, lifts its mighty head of vivid green above the scene.

About the house and outbuildings and drive there is a fine rising sweep of turf dominated by a great coppice of *Rhododendron arboreum;* there are borders of fine shrubs and herbaceous perennials, splendid specimens of Irish yew—Annes Grove has a claim to own the mother-plant of this fine form. Of the plants against the walls of house and outbuildings, the most striking are, perhaps, the grand specimens of *Callistemon*—scarlet, crimson, or yellow-flowered bottle-brush bushes of Australia; and a *Rosa bracteata*, the Macartney Rose, evergreen, tender, and to my mind the most superb species of its genus, especially for the cup-shape of its wonderfully substantial, pure white flowers.

In the walled garden the good rule of expectation and surprise has been respected by dividing the area into enclosures with yew hedges. The parterres, some of them box-edged, are planted with a wide range of herbaceous perennials, and there are two fine, straight, hedge-backed herbaceous borders. But there are shrubs here also, *Hydrangea villosa*—nowhere else have I seen this species as fine as it is in the gardens of Co. Cork, and notably at Ardsallagh—and, for example, *Eucryphia moorei*, tenderest of its genus and one of the prettiest. Among the perennials most striking to the English eye are the *Thalictrum dipterocarpum* of a size which they do not attain in England, vast heads of pale mauve and yellow flowers to a height of eight or nine feet; *Melianthus major* for its superb glaucous leaves; and *Kirengishoma palmata* with its campanulate yellow flowers at a season, October, when flowers are not so plentiful.

The yew hedges at Annes Grove are far from sombre for they are everywhere grown through and over by the flame-flowered *Tropaeolium speciosum*, the perennial "nasturtium" which is naturalised there. This area of the garden also encloses a little water and rock garden of both aquatic and alpine plants including dwarf shrubs. The walls, too, are richly

Annes Grove in Co. Cork was the creation of Mr. Richard Grove Annesley, who died in 1966.
For over fifty years Mr. Annesley not only added to his own remarkable garden, but helped
in the creation of other Irish gardens, notably, Ilnacullin.

One of the river vistas in the lower garden at Annes Grove.

planted, one notable plant being a *Vitis coigentiae* which sometimes seeds itself so that small vines appear even in the crevices between paving stones.

These are my general impressions of, and attempt to convey the shape of, Annes Grove. I want now to refer to Mr R. C. Jenkinson, again in the *Journal* of the Royal Horticultural Society, whose observations on Irish gardens are so valuable for my purpose here. He is chiefly concerned with the plants of outstanding quality and interest, and like me he was much struck with the beauty of the big *Cornus contraversa variegata* which, half a dozen years ago, was thirty-three feet tall. For my part, I have never seen so fine a specimen anywhere else.

He too, again, notes the almost incredible size and excellence of the *Thalictrum dipterocarpum* in the walled garden; but he also notes what I missed, for example the scarlet-flowered amaryllis *Hippeastrum* x *ackermanii* and the lovely mauve-flowered *Anemone obtusiloba patula* which I cannot even persuade to come up at all. Mr Jenkinson names a few of the outstandingly good rhododendrons at Annes Grove (*Journal* R.H.S. Vol. LXXXIVZ. October 1959). Among the watergarden plants he distinguishes *Lysichitum americanum* and *L. campschatcense, Primula rosea, Orontium aquaticum*. On the great bank over the valley, he picks out two barberries for special mention, *Berberis francisci-ferdinandi* for

The native ferns are used as understorey plants in deep shade.

its vivid autumn colour and fruit, and *B. calliantha* for its splendid evergreen foliage. Also, one olearea, *O. ilicifolia* which is indeed a splendid plant, like a very fine silver holly.

Is any general impression possible? Yes, I think so: curiously enough, although this is a large garden and not, excepting in some of the deeper woodland parts, troubled by the shut-in feeling which can be oppressive, there is an impression of intimacy, of secrecy. I wrote elsewhere* that whereas the gardens of Latin Europe are conceived and designed as settings for human intercourse and human attitudinising, the great "English"—in this case Irish—paradise gardens are for looking at, that is they are justified not for their use, like a work of architecture, but of themselves, like a work of fine art.

Annes Grove is very much such a paradise garden. But it is one which has been modified by the influence of, and a very civilized feeling for, more formal styles.

The English Garden by Edward Hyams, London, 1964.

4

Glenveagh Castle

I "discovered" the great gardens of Glenveagh Castle in 1962. Nobody had told me about them, I just, as it were, fell over them. The Republic has a most wonderful way, despite the splendid efforts of the Bord Failte, of hiding its best and softly denying its existence, a perversity which, while entertaining, can also be exasperating. But I fancy that in the case of Glenveagh it is rather a matter of the owner valuing his privacy; and who shall blame him?

I had made my way to the south-west and then northward through the west, and all that lovely country where sea and land are mingled in land-and-seascape like none other known to me anywhere in the world, where, in late summer, gorse and heather paint the hillsides purple and gold; where the hedges are of fuchsia or hebe; and where you repeatedly have to drive many miles inland to get to a place which is fifty yards away across water. I had, too, climbed the strange, ash-grey mountains of county Clare and sat down for two hours to contemplate, with awe-struck satisfaction, the mighty cliffs of Moher, for there is one of the most majestic stretches of coastal scenery in the world. The hills of Clare fascinated me as very few countrysides have done: from a distance they seem all naked stone in a pattern of vertically set slices most pleasing to the eye: but when you get into them you find the lower slopes very rich in a peculiar and quite local alpine flora. There I had found acres of Mountain Aven, *Dryas octopetala*, Burnet Rose, Winter Green, and the gorgeous Bloody Cranesbill. But I had gone on and on, then rested for a day or two in the most pleasant of small Irish towns I know, Dumfanaghy, in Co. Donegal, with its countryside of emerald turf blue-starred in autumn with small gentians, and its miles of empty golden sands haunted by the pleasant calling of oyster-catchers.

It was, then, from Dumfanaghy that I discovered Glenveagh. It was a barman in the "snug" I frequented who said that if it was gardens I wanted, they had one. I am grateful to him even if he did, by misdirecting me how to get to it with the blessing which one

Glenveagh Castle, expressive of the remoteness and privacy of this great far-western garden in Co. Donegal.

comes to expect in the far west, send me driving over a most villainous road for mile after mile across an unpeopled peat bog. Then came the business of negotiating with the strict guardians of the Castle's privacy. It is a thing I am entirely in favour of: no garden is really large enough for more than one person at a time. However, hospitality overcame the wish to keep the garden as private as it is, by nature and situation, remote and difficult of access.

The Castle itself, nineteenth century Romantic and superbly matching its site — a baroque house would look ridiculous in such country — stands on Loch Veagh with, beyond the water, the Derry Veagh Mountains folding sweetly down to the stillness of that lovely, narrow lake. The gardens are laid out about and on the hillside above the castle; and the present gardener, owner of this domain set so privately between peat-bog, water, and mountain, is Mr Henry P. Mc Ilhenny who spends much of the spring and summer there, while at other seasons he is at his other home in America where his collection and knowledge of Impressionist paintings are famous. What Mr Mc Ilhenny had to start with at Glenveagh was a garden already made by a notable gardener, but thereafter, and by force of circumstances, neglected.

Glenveagh is a garden of half a dozen styles nicely united into an integral work. At its heart, in the near neighbourhood of the house, Italianate, French and formal English styles predominate. But in the skirts of the garden, where it runs into the wild, the arts of woodland and alpine gardening have been used. It is much less a Robinsonian garden than any of those yet discussed. Its principal parts are an Italian garden; an English flower garden a little in the manner of Gertrude Jekyll I suppose, but still more in a style of nineteenth century flower gardening which was developed in Ireland itself; an area of fine lawn, trees and shrub-borders known as the Pleasure Garden; and the Wild Garden.

The Pleasure Garden alone would repay some days of slow and careful contemplation. The vast lawn is of such turf as is only to be found in Ireland, its green almost too intense. The shape of this lawn is irregular rather as if it were a lake with a natural basin. It reminded me of a theory which I believe is my own, that level lawns in Irish as in English gardens are, like the raked sand expanses of certain Japanese gardens, really water-substitutes, doing much the same office as small lakes in gardens, resting the eye and providing a foil for such less tranquil elements as are provided by the shapes of trees and bushes and rocks, and such exciting elements as are provided by the colours of flowers and the shapes of buildings. The surroundings of this lake-like lawn, which is backed by stately trees, are groups and borders of shrubs, and some rocky outcrops gardened with alpine and other plants rather in the manner of the Rowallane garden. Among these, rather surprisingly in a region of such heavy rainfall and of soil so kind to such ericaceous and American plants as detest lime, are *Cistus* in variety and that strange bromeliad, *Rhodostachys pitcairnensis*.

Glenveagh Castle. In some Irish gardens lawns are used as lake substitutes. In the background, the Derryveagh Mountains.

Among the notable plants of this area of the gardens are magnificently grown camellias, rhododendrons, including members of the tender and fragrant-flowered *maddenii* series, some fine hebes, the shrubby veronicas of New Zealand, well-grown eucryphias of all the known species and their hybrids excepting, I think, *E. cordifolia*, eucalyptus and oleareas. Here, as in other Irish gardens, *Crinodendron* reaches a stature and fulness which is not to be found in English gardens, and the hundred-inch rainfall which coddles them likewise favours such giant-leaved and stately primitives of the genus *Rhododendron* as *R. falconeri*, *R. macabeanum*, *R. sinogrande* and their allies. Since my personal taste favours the rare flowering shrubs above all other groups or categories of plants for gardens, the most pleasing of the Glenveagh spectacles to me was that provided by clumps of well-grown *Olearea semidentata* in bloom. Glenveagh is one of the very few gardens known to me where this Australasian bush with its beautifully glaucous foliage, the leaves handsomely felted on the underside, and its great mauve-centred daisies, is at home.

Above and dominating the lawn and its surrounding plantings is a long terrace-walk gardened with *Pernettya*, *Rhododendron* again—I don't know how many of its thousand species are represented but the azalea series is there in variety—*Acacia*, and I mean the true acacias, not *Robinia*—and exotic *Sorbi*, all these underplanted with choice groundlings. It is from this level that you begin the climb into the mountain-woodland garden, or wild

One of the formal features of an informal garden — the dolphin fountain at Glenveagh.

Glenveagh, where in the old Irish garden useful and ornamental plants are mingled.

garden, partly by narrow woodland paths. One very pleasing and original feature is that the steps are built into what I can only describe as a torrent of huge granite boulders which form the tumbled face of the hill and are pleasingly overgrown with vividly green mosses of many species. They are also rich in both native and exotic ferns and heaths which grow naturally in the crevices between the rocks, and to these Mr Mc Ilhenny has added, with admirable gardening art, a considerable number of the dwarf, miniature-leaved rhododendrons which are the "heather", as it were, of certain parts of the Himalayas—a technique first used by Colonel Messel of Nymans fame.

Still above the gardened, hilly woodland rises a flight of wide and steep granite steps, sixty of them, so steep that the climb is slightly trying to anyone who suffers from vertigo. These lead you to a formal and very simply grassed belvedere contained in clipped hedges of *Rhododendron ponticum*. This is an admirable feature of the gardens, for the height enables one to enjoy a magnificent view of the castle, the gardens, part of Loch Veagh, and the lovely violet-brown backcloth of the Derryveagh mountains, screen folding down upon screen of hills in one of the most beautiful scenic patterns I have ever seen.

From this height you descend to the Flower Garden, which is also a Kitchen Garden, a rectangular area of considerable extent, contained in good walls and laid out geometrically. There are some shrubs, including roses, but the principal interest in this part is provided by herbaceous perennials. This garden is backed by the castle walls, on which are a lean-to

Glenveagh,
the remote
and beautiful
garden main-
tained by Mr.
Henry Mc Ilhenny
in Co. Donegal.

Glenveagh. In the foreground a planting of lilies; beyond, the conservatory and a propagation house against the castle wall.

greenhouse for propagation, and a handsome semi-circular conservatory for tender exotics. In the Flower Garden borders the *auratum* and the Chinese trumpet lilies flourish as they do in few gardens, and in the mild, moist air the scent of the *auratums* is almost overwhelming.

Finally, I must say something about the "Italian" garden. The term "Italian Garden", while it does at once invoke an image of a certain kind of garden in which evergreens, some clipped, others growing free, stonework, and cypresses predominate and flowers are few, is really rather a loose one. There is, for example, a world of difference between the Tuscan Humanist style inspired by the poet-gardener Petrarch, himself inspired by an imperfect idea of what the ancient Roman gardens were like, and the style of the grand Roman Renaissance gardens.* The Italian garden at Glenveagh is more or less in the tradition of the North Italian Humanist gardens, small, simple, enclosed, paved; it has its clipped evergreens, some topiary work which is not over-elaborate, some good statuary, and more flowers, perhaps, than would be the case in a classic Tuscan garden. It is, at all events, a pretty and very pleasant corner and it serves to illustrate my point that all the traditions and styles of European garden art are to be found in the Irish garden, just as much modified as is necessary to "naturalise" them into the Irish scene.

Italian Gardens by Georgina Masson.

5

Ilnacullin

Less famous than Bantry Bay in the west of Ireland, itself high on the list of the world's most beautiful bays, but not, to my mind, less lovely, is the Bay of Glengariff. This bay, with its water so richly blue in fine weather, its surface stippled with small islands, and its shores variously green with the foliage of the fine woods which grow almost down to the water, is an enchanted and enchanting place for those who find pleasure in geographical harmonies.

One of the islands in this bay is called Garinish or, more correctly so I have been told, Ilnacullin. It first entered history, and the knowledge of anyone beyond the neighbourhood of Glengariff, when belatedly, in 1815, a martello tower was built on its highest point as part of that chain of such small fortresses which were Britain's "Maginot Line" against a feared Napoleonic invasion. Presumably this building must have been done between Bonaparte's escape from Elba and the Battle of Waterloo; there would have been no point in it before or after, although come to think of it the War Office is apt to overlook such trivialities as that. Moreover, the little fortress was garrisoned, for some mysterious reason, until 1825 — no doubt the War Office had overlooked it. Then, however, the ten men and one officer composing the garrison were withdrawn and the island reverted to its ancient state — rock, peat, and a small population of goats which could find nourishment on its wretched vegetation. And so it remained until, in 1910, it was bought from the War Office by Mr Annan Bryce who wanted to build a house on it and make himself a garden. He was very much keener on the garden than on the house, for all his early work went into garden-making, and the building of the house was repeatedly postponed. To advise him about the design of the garden, as well as to design him a house, Bryce called in Harold Peto: the result was one of the most successful of the many unpromising partnerships in the history of garden art. As Dr H. R. Fletcher put it (*Journal*, R.H.S., January, 1966):

"Peto climbed to the Martello tower, gazed around and, I suppose very naturally

Ilnacullin. This garden is superbly sited on the Island of Garinish in the Bay of Glengariff.

for him, advised on the creation on this great island rock of a formal Italianate Garden. Remarkably enough Mr Bryce appears not to have thought Peto had taken complete leave of his senses and, until 1924, when Annan Bryce died (except for a break from 1914-1918 during the First World War), these two men combined their ideas and resources in the creation of this formal architectural garden with beautifully placed colonnades, flights of steps, terraces and pools, all of which blend in remarkably well with the natural setting and with the surrounding informal plantings. An Italian teahouse of Bath stone, and an Italian temple; columns of "Rosso Antico" taken from a rediscovered quarry and of a beautiful red colour; marble slabs, white and thickly veined with a rich yellow, from the island of Scyros; Carrara marble balustrading; a floor of green Connemara marble done in scagliola, the work of Italians brought over for the purpose, these are some of the architectural features. . . ."

Since Ilnacullin is an important example of Peto's work something should be said about the man himself. H. A. Peto was born in 1854 and died in 1933. He was a successful professional architect well-known for his Italianate taste which he had presumably acquired when visiting Italy as a young man. In particular he was a great advocate of the Italian style for garden design and architecture, and to these styles he was faithful when he began to receive commissions to design gardens not only in Britain but in the south of France. His own garden, which he made at Iford near Bradford-on-Avon, was a model of the Humanist garden, modified for English conditions, but Ilnacullin is perhaps his master-piece. He was not, I think, actively hostile to the Robinsonian wild gardening which dominated his epoch, but he deprecated its excesses and he believed that the formal styles could coexist with it and ought not to be neglected. He was, in fact, one of the two or three men who made sure that these styles were not lost to English and Irish gardens.

We know nothing of Annan Bryce's own ideas as a gardener, but it is safe bet that, without Peto's influence, they would have been Robinsonian, for Bryce belonged to the class of rich men with country houses who were all, at that time, making exotic woodland gardens under the influence of Gravetye, Nymans, Mount Usher. Probably, moreover, his mind would have been turned to plantsmanship by realising that the mild and moist climate of Ilnacullin and its peaty soil — of which more had to be imported from the mainland before much planting could be done — and freedom from frost in all but the mildest winters, made it possible to grow tender exotics of the kind which, until Colonel Messel at Nymans and the Walpoles at Mount Usher showed the way with their plantings, were associated only with the uniquely mild climate of Tresco in the Scilly Islands.

The result of the happy working partnership between Bryce and Peto was, and still

At Ilnacullin, designed by Harold Peto, Italianate and English romantic styles are combined successfully.

is, a formal garden set in and inextricably blended with a semi-wild plantsman's garden, the whole, again, inextricably blended into a half-terrestrial, half-maritime and wholly lovely natural scene. Ilnacullin is a gem of art set in a jewel of nature. And, happily, Annan Bryce's son and heir, Roland L'Estrange Bryce, was as much attached to Ilnacullin as his father had been, and as determined to continue and perfect the work. It was he who at last built the house which his father, absorbed in the garden, had never got round to. And he continued the planting of the gardens with the advice of such knowledgeable friends as Mr Richard Grove Annesley—quite a lot of Ilnacullin plants came from Annes Grove in the first place. Finally, as an Irish patriot, Bryce left the island garden and house to the Republic when he died: it was his wish that it become the Chequers, as it were, of the Irish Presidents. This has never happened, but Ilnacullin is now the responsibility of the Commissioners of Public Works and more specifically of their principal architect, himself a remarkable gardener, Mr S. F. Maskell. Fortunately for Mr Maskell and the Commissioners, Bryce's head gardener, Mr R. Mackenzie, "went with" the property. As a consequence of Mr Maskell's and Mr Mackenzie's skills and hard work, Ilnacullin is impeccably gardened.

The garden is centred on the formal Italianate part, a regular paved area about a large formal sheet of water, contained between raised, Renaissance, colonnaded pavilions at each end and dense plantings of shrubs and trees at the sides. The south-western pavilion has been wonderfully well sited so as to frame, and so draw into the garden, some of the loveliest coastal scenery in Europe, a pattern of sparkling water, small coves, promontories and islands, subtly linked to the garden by declining banks, with shrubs and trees down to the very sea.

In 1959 Mr R. C. Jenkinson visited Ilnacullin and wrote a short account of the garden for the *Journal* of the Royal Horticultural Society. Among the plants of exceptional interest which he noted (*R.H.S. Journal*, Pt.10 V.84) were the fine representatives of the *grande* series of rhododendrons, the giant leaved and tree-like species of the genus; some of the rare oleareas, notably *O. myrsinoides* in a very large specimen; tender rhododendrons of the *cinnabarinum* series; *Taiwania cryptermeroides* and *Dacridium cupressinum*, two very rare southern hemisphere trees, and then some others equally rare—*Athrotaxis laxifolius, Callitris oblonga* and *C. cupressoides*. He was also greatly taken with some of Ilnacullin's myrtles as I was when I saw *Myrtus ugni* and *M. lechleriana*, and the much more commonly planted *M. luma* in flower there in spring; and again, in late summer or early autumn, in fruit. *Myrtus lechleriana*, in particular, was notable, an eight feet tall and neatly symmetrical shrub, the flowers casting their strong and spicy scent to a considerable distance, the fruits black shot with mahogany-red lights. These fruits turned out on tasting to be as palatable as the better-known fruits of *M. ugni* which Queen Victoria is said to have relished.

At Ilnacullin, as at Mount Usher, past accounts enable one to make comparisons with

Ilnacullin. Many of the garden walks terminate in fine views of Glengariff Bay.

the present state of the garden and so to judge its progress. Mr Jenkinson, in the R.H.S. account to which the reader has already been referred, gives estimates of the size attained by certain rare plants in the garden — for example, *Dacrydium kirkii*, *Phyllocladus glaucus*, *Agathis australis* and *Acacia riceana*. The visitor of ten years later can see for himself how these exotic rarities continue to prosper in a soil as artificially provided as that of the one other, and very different, garden known to me which can be compared with this one — that of the Isola Bella in Lake Maggiore, comparable at least in the sense that it, too, was made on an originally naked rock, that its native style was the inspiration of Ilnacullin's 'Italianate' buildings, and that it is planted with tender exotics.

For Ilnacullin, as for Mount Usher, one could publish lists of names of rare exotics to fill pages of this book. They help to bear out my argument that in the Irish paradise gardens what have been achieved and are presented are scenes from an ideal, a possible world — the essence of romance. And that this has been done by bringing together nature's masterpieces in the kingdom of the plants, the exceptionally beautiful and curious trees and shrubs and herbs from all over the world. I do not know whether Australasia, the Americas, Europe, Africa or Asia be the best represented in the borders, shrubberies and arboreta of Ilnacullin; but I do know that one has no feeling of being in a mere botanical garden inspecting a collection. Plants have not been used by the Bryces for their own sake any more than rare pigments were used by some of the Old Masters of painting for their own sake; they were used to obtain a particular effect or to enhance a feeling of riches in the whole. In the first article I ever wrote about Ilnacullin I made the point that the counties of West Cork and Kerry are themselves natural gardens of enchanting beauty — rock and bog, stream and mountain, embellished by the flaming gold of rock-hugging gorse, the rich purple of heather, the softer colour of ling, the manifold greens and forms of foliage. As well as the native flora there is a perfectly naturalised one, now also native, of fuchsia, hebe, rhododendron and monbretia. But there is, on Illnacullin, no abrupt passage from the formal to the unplanted but lovely wild, and the vast range of exotics is integrated into the picture so that not even the most rare and curious tree is simply a specimen; it, too, is an element.

In the matter of growth if not of range, Ilnacullin is very remarkable for its Australian and New Zealand plants. The acacias — florists' "mimosa" — leptospermums, callistemons and their allies, which can be more or less grown in our own milder countries, here attain in a very short time a stature and a luxuriance which are, apparently, uncommon even in their own country. Never elsewhere have I seen the great New Zealand forget-me-not, *Myosotidium nobile* growing so lush and strong. *Lomatia ferruginea* is happy here. The extraordinary number of *Olearea* species can be equalled, in Europe, only by the special collection at Malahide Castle. How I envied the splendid plants of, for example, *Drimys colorata* with

Ilnacullin.
Harold Peto's
Italianate
pavilion and
lily pool,
which is the
heart of
Ilnacullin
on Garinish
Island.

Ilnacullin is remarkable for perfectly accomplished combinations of stone and live plant material.

its curious gold and garnet leaves, the embothriums, the boronias, grevilleas and myrtles. Many of the exotics seed themselves naturally, including callistemons, cryptomerias, leptospermums and hoherias. Agapanthus and watsonia are as perfectly at home here as on their native veldt. The tree-ferns *Dicksonia* look like part of the wild flora, and even the incomparably lovely tree-fern *Cyathea dealbata*, the underside of the mighty fronds a lovely silver-blue, are doing well, although for this species there is no garden to compare with Rossdohan.

The finest of all the St John's Worts, *Hypericum* x 'Rowallane' here attain seven or eight feet and bear thousands of the large golden cup-flowers. Among the great rarities not named by Mr Jenkinson are *Bowkeria gerardiana* and *Virgilia capensis*.

I must leave it to William MacQuitty's photographs to show how all this plant material has been composed into a work of art. Owing, I think, to Harold Peto's restraining hand, there is no muddle anywhere in this garden: one wanders at random but always by fine

A lawn vista at Ilnacullin from one of Harold Peto's Italianate pavilions.

broad paths, each with its vista, among the plantings. And not one of these paths makes the mistake of going nowhere, every walk has its termination either in one of Peto's works, or — and here the nature of the site has great advantages — you emerge on to soft turf and heath and rock overlooking a little beach and commanding one of the many lovely views of Glengariff Bay.

To sum up: Ilnacullin offers four major satisfactions of the highest order to the lover of natural beauty worked on by art: an exceptionally successful Italianate garden of rich stones finely wrought and of good plants skilfully chosen and grown; this set in a frame of wild garden planted with the most beautiful trees and shrubs from all over the world; this, again, set in an outer frame of rare natural beauty composed of sea and mountains; and all composing an integral work of art.

I cannot offer comparison with other gardens by way of guidance: there is no other garden like this one.

6

Rossdohan

When I first wrote and published a short account of Ilnacullin—which I then called Garinish—I got into trouble with the men of Cork, a fiery race, for misplacing it into Co. Kerry. Rossdohan, interesting principally for its extraordinary tropical air, really is in Kerry. An island, but technically rather than effectively so, for you can drive on to it by a causeway, it is virtually a part of the Parknasilla peninsula, one of those long fingers of land which south-west Ireland thrusts out into the Atlantic. Its climate, as to temperature and humidity, is much the same as Ilnacullin's or perhaps even a shade milder in severe winters, that is to say it is very nearly frost-free and snow is extremely rare and never heavy. But in one respect, and this has proved of almost fatal consequence, it is very inferior: Ilnacullin is, for some reason which I confess I have not studied, shielded from the worst violence of the terrific south-westerly and westerly gales which are the bane of all Atlantic coast gardens and which, for example, do so much damage at, and necessitate massive windbreak planting on, Tresco, to protect the famous sub-tropical Abbey Gardens. Rossdohan has no such natural protection as Ilnacullin. It is completely exposed, and that exposure has wrecked the garden more than once. It is fortunate that the Australasian genera for which it is so remarkable are very wind-tolerant. But the garden is even now being recovered by its owners from the chaos wrought by the most recent gale disasters.

It should be said at once that Rossdohan would not, by many people, be called a garden at all; and it is not, in the sense that Ilnacullin decidedly is, a garden in the formal meaning of the word. It is very remarkable for its plants and for the subtropical "feeling" or "atmosphere"; but it was never really designed, it was just planted. It is as if its planter was an instrument of nature but one which had intelligence and could select what, if not how, he planted. Entirely artificial—for originally it was peat-covered rock with a single hawthorn tree—yet it seems to be a piece of natural woodland displaced from somewhere in Australasia.

Rossdohan. This garden in Co. Kerry has the finest examples of the tree fern family to be seen in Europe. *Dicksonia* is there naturalised.

The first maker of this garden, as I shall continue to call it despite what I have just said, was Samuel Thomas Heard, Surgeon-Major (Ret.) Indian Army, who bought the island of Rossdohan in the year 1870. He built an extremely handsome house on a sort of rocky promontory, so that it is almost surrounded by the sea. At some time between then and now this house was gutted by fire, but its impressive shell still stands and I suppose that the interior and the roof could be restored. The present owners have, however, preferred to build two new bungalows in a more convenient part of the grounds.

Heard's first care was to plant a windbreak. It would have been quite impossible to succeed at Rossdohan without some such protection from the south-west; even as it is the garden has, as I said, repeatedly been destroyed by gales. According to such sources as are available, and from observation, the plants used to form this windbreak were *Cupressus macrocarpa*, *Pinus radiata*, the tall Irish gorse, and two shrubs, escallonia and *Rhododendron ponticum*. Now the use of the pine and the rhododendron in this list suggests to me that

The underside of the giant fronds of the tree fern *Cyathea dealbata* is silver-blue.

Within the shelter, and in fact long before that shelter can possibly have been fully effective, Heard began to plant, and he concentrated most of his attention on Australasian species. Why? Again, it is a guess, but I think he must have had Tresco in mind. We know how well these plants did there: a note in the *Gardeners Chronicle* in the year 1906 Heard had studied Augustus Smith's problem and solution on Tresco in the Scillies. Smith and his successor had been coping with the business of protecting the garden they were making from the same gales since 1834, and Heard did not start work until 1870. As a matter of fact the pine in question has not proved very satisfactory in either place; on Tresco and at Rossdohan they are blown over in hundreds. A great deal of what remained of Heard's original windbreak trees were destroyed by one of the worst gales of modern times in 1957. The present owners Mr P. and Mr R. J. Walker, who are brothers, are now replanting and have been doing so for ten years, but this time they are using *Pinus muricata*, which has a firmer hold on the ground and is, perhaps, less top-heavy than *P. radiata*.

(Vol.40. p.368), dealing with a visit to Heard's garden, mentions several species and in some cases gives their stature at Rossdohan. The genera include *Eucalyptus, Acacia, Melaleuca, Hakea, Agonis, Kunzea, Callistemon, Boronia, Pittosporum*. It is odd, as will appear, that it does not mention tree-ferns. Although Heard did give most of his attention and space to these Australasian genera, he was not a rigid specialist and the same note mentions South American, South African, Chinese and Japanese genera. Commenting on this note and on his own visit to Rossdohan sixty years later (R.H.S. *Journal*, Part I, Vol. XCI), Dr H. R. Fletcher says:

"Not all the plants mentioned by Watson were seen during the half-day visit in May, and some may not now be there. On the other hand a great many plants not recorded by Watson *were* noted, and presumably these were rather young things in 1906 or have since been planted. What a pity it is that the planting records in so many gardens have been lost and that we thus do not know the age of so many remarkable trees and shrubs in cultivation.

"Surely *Myrtus luma* and *Clethra arborea* must have been at Rossdohan in 1906; maybe they were too common for Watson to comment on them . . . they are in astonishing numbers, the former well over twenty feet and the latter over forty feet, and self-sown seedlings are some of the commonest weeds in the place. Almost as common is the Australian Blackwood Acacia, *A. melanoxylon;* several specimens are at least fifty feet tall and one or two must be close on seventy feet with stems over a foot in diameter at breast height. They flower in April, and when draped with pale yellow they must be a beautiful sight. Self-sown seedlings of all sizes and ages are there in their thousands. And likewise in their thousands are seedlings of the Tasmanian and Australian Musk Wood, *Olearia argyrophylla,* which was scarcely in flower though covered with numerous corymbose flower heads. When a thirty-feet plant is covered with countless six-inch flower heads of white and yellow florets it is an attractive sight, and there are many such plants at Rossdohan, some with stems twelve to eighteen inches in diameter. . . ."

Dr Fletcher then introduced the subject of *Mitrarea coccinea* which is to be found clambering over the ramifications of many of the other plants at Rossdohan.

"Not only on the stems of the *Olearia* does this plant climb; it can be seen stretching to a height of thirty feet up a sixty-foot stem of *Acacia melanoxylon*. Astonishing.

"Several Eucalypts have attained great size. The specimen of *Eucalyptus globulus* approaching ninety feet in height and as much in branch spread, has a

Rossdohan. Detail of *Cyathea dealbata* frond measuring about fifteen feet.

trunk seventeen feet in circumference at three feet; another, rather taller, has a girth of fourteen feet eight inches. *E. coccifera* and *E. viminalis* must be eighty feet high, the latter with a stem diameter of two feet at breast height. As these also regenerate freely, clearly the conditions are agreeable for the cultivation of many more species of this remarkable genus; in fact several other species have been planted, including *E. perriniana, resinifera, simondsii* and *pauciflora.*''

What is the general effect of all this? It is that of an idealised southern hemisphere Eden, for despite the presence of Far Eastern and European species, the Australasians and South Americans dominate the scene completely. Had Adam been created south of the Equator then this, perhaps, is what paradise would have looked like. I have not, of course, given a full list of the plants cited by Dr Fletcher: the reader will have had enough of Latin names, and the kind of plants we are dealing with at Rossdohan, very rare in gardens, have no English vernacular names.

For my part, and although I was impressed and delighted with hundreds of the plants I saw at Rossdohan, what really took my fancy, what made this wild garden thrust out into the Atlantic so evocative of boyhood dreams of coral islands and tropical explorations — our dreams were confined to earth in those days — were the ferns. And not only the exotics, for such natives as Hart's Tongue, Lady Fern, Male Fern and even the commonest polypody are here so large and flourishing as to look exotic themselves. Still, the exotics, such as woodwardias, are more impressive, and above all the tree-ferns for which this garden is very remarkable.

The only tree fern which is not uncommon in Irish, Cornish and West Scottish gardens, is *Dicksonia antarctica,* a New Zealander which is not hopelessly tender and will, indeed, stand some snow and a few degrees of frost. These dicksonias in many English West Country gardens as far east as the Dart estuary survived, albeit damaged, the atrocious winter of 1962/3. This tree-fern, attaining a height of ten or twelve feet, with a trunk sometimes up to seven or eight feet, is quite literally a weed at Rossdohan, the sporelings springing up in thousands and in the most unlikely places. But what is much more remarkable — and I recorded my own delighted surprise at it some six years before Dr Fletcher's similar reaction was published in the R.H.S. *Journal,* is that *Cyathea dealbata,* a far more beautiful tree-fern and extremely rare in cultivation, is almost as flourishing. To the best of my belief this glorious feature of Rossdohan is unique. There are one or two cyatheas elsewhere but nothing like the great cyatheas of Rossdohan. Here is what Dr Fletcher has to say about them:

"Nowhere else have I seen this most beautiful of Tree Ferns growing out of doors (although Messrs Walker have generously and sensibly given young plants to

Rossdohan. A view of the more formal part of the garden, principally remarkable for a wealth of Australian and New Zealand plants, and particularly for tree ferns, not only the relatively hardy *Dicksonia*, but for the far more beautiful and tender *Cyathea dealbata*.

Rossdohan, where fern sporelings flourish by the thousand.

other gardens in Southern Ireland in the hope that the species may become established in cultivation elsewhere). Mature plants at Rossdohan are almost as common as dicksonias — and far more beautiful — stems up to five to six feet and great fronds, sometimes over ten feet long, green or bluish-green above and wonderfully silvery below; not so large as in the native habitat on the North and middle islands of New Zealand, but how impressive. What a pity it is that we do not know when and how *Cyathea dealbata*, usually grown as an evergreen warm greenhouse fern, became established in the open garden at Rossdohan.''

It is worth going a long way to stand under one of the great umbrella canopies formed by these ferns, and to look up at the very beautiful but quite indescribable silver-blue of the undersides of the fronds.

North American conifers, Asiatic palms and Australasian tree ferns in effective combination at Rossdohan.

At first glance, a New Zealand gorge; Rossdohan is exceptionally rich in Australasian plants.

Rossdohan was bought by the Walkers in 1955 and the work they are doing there, much of it with their own hands, is a noble one. They had spent two years clearing fallen trees from the garden, rescuing hundreds of rare and lovely plants from the mass of derelict timber, when in 1957 a gale blew down another thousand trees. It is amazing that the Walkers were not discouraged, but the work goes on, the windbreak is being restored, and even with a great many fallen trees littering the place, as there were when I first saw it, Rossdohan is one of the most exciting wild gardens known to me. As I have already said, many people would not allow it to be a garden at all, for there is nowhere a touch of formal arrangement. But, wild woodland though it be, transposed from 40 degrees South to 51 degrees North, it is, after all, a product of art and science "after Nature".

7

Fota

Fota, world-famous among dendrologists, is the third of the island gardens of Ireland, although again only technically an island since it can be reached on foot or on wheels by a causeway. Although its feature of greatest importance is its trees, it is not simply an arboretum, but a garden-cum-park. It is worth noting here that the use of the word garden always gives rise to some uncertainty: virtually all large Irish gardens are what the French would call a park. I call Fota a garden in the broadest sense, but although when I first saw it the strictly "garden" part, that is the walled enclosures, were still very much flower gardens, they have to some extent been turned over to the growing of vegetables since then, so that the part which is really a gentleman's park, always the more important, is now more so than ever.

Fota is in Cobh Harbour, east along the coast from the city of Cork, and it resembles neither Rossdohan nor Ilnacullin. It is not a wild garden and there is very little about it that could be called Robinsonian. It is in fact extremely difficult either to describe or to photograph, and the reason for this is that it makes magnificent use of *space* — great sweeps of grass, framed in distant trees and accented only by an urn or a statue, giving an impression of grand repose which is most pleasing; but space, on that scale, with the, as it were, retaining features always distant, is the reverse of photogenic.

These great sweeps of grass defined by trees are to some extent in the English eighteenth-century "landskip" style; and yet that will not do after all, for although there are echoes of "Capability" Brown, yet the very broad, straight walks, lightly ornamented with stonework kerbs and such objects as fine stone vases, give to the whole a very French look, even a faint suggestion of the style of Le Nôtre. There is nothing Italianate about this garden, and the transition from the park to the garden proper is from the grand manner of France superimposed on English landscape, to the typical Anglo-Irish style of the nineteenth-century walled garden.

Fota. The park of this great semi-formal garden constitutes one of the most remarkable arboreta in Europe.

The laying out of the gardens, making of terraces and building of high walls were all done in the first half of the nineteenth century by James Hugh Smith Barry, and as far as is known he did not have the advice of a specialist, nor were any drawings made by a garden architect, or, if there were any, they have not survived. It seems to me that the planting of the very fine yew hedges, pierced by doorways made of fine stone piers carrying handsome wrought-iron gates, may well date from the same epoch, although such hedges do not in fact take so long to reach a massive maturity as is commonly supposed. For example, the yew hedges at Sissinghurst Castle in Kent, which look so very ancient, had reached that appearance within twenty years of being planted. At all events, the yew hedges of Fota serve to divide certain parts of the garden into enclosures, thus ensuring the element of "expectation and surprise" which Lawrence Johnson made such a point of at Hidcote Barton Manor. Smith Barry also planted the deep-shelter belts, which do something to protect Fota from the south-westerlies, and some of the magnificent conifers, chiefly his silver firs, for which Fota is celebrated.

Smith Barry died in 1857 and was succeeded by his fourteen-year-old nephew and ward who later became Lord Barrymore. The boy had already caught his uncle's interest in trees and other plants, and he very soon began planting, continuing Smith Barry's policy but broadening the range. He continued in this course until his death in 1915, so that he was adding to Fota's collection of trees and shrubs for over half a century. Mr R. C. Jenkinson, writing about Fota in the *Journal* of the Royal Horticultural Society, suggests that since, between about 1875 and 1900, Lord Barrymore and Lord Annesley of Castlewellan were both importing rare plants from Japan, they probably exchanged both plants and ideas. Barrymore also exchanged plants and seeds with another notable plantsman Lord Headfort. Among his friends was Sir Frederick Moore who played such an important part in the making of Mount Usher. Moore, and Lady Moore were also—Lady Moore still is—friends of the Hon. Mrs Dorothy Ball who, with her husband Major Ball, are the present owners of Fota.

I will first say something about the plants which made the most impression on me when I visited Fota. I find I have starred notes of a very fine specimen of *Lomatia ferruginea* with its finely divided bronze foliage and its masses of strange, grevillea-like flowers; of desfontaineas very remarkable for their great size and good flourishing condition; of a handsome young *Pinus montezumae* of which Mrs Ball complained that it was not as glaucous as the Mount Usher form; of an enormous *Eucalyptus coccifera*—there can be no doubt that Ireland could grow eucalyptus on a commercial scale. Further notes mention the largest specimen of *Drimys aromatica* I have ever seen, palms and dracaenas—plants related to the astonishing Dragon Tree of the Canary Islands, among which the mighty plant at Icod was said to be 14,000 years old and whose hollow trunk was first a Guanche temple and later a

At Fota, formal and informal elements combine to express the unique character of the Irish garden.

Christian chapel. Another record-breaker of great beauty at Fota is an *Arbutus menziesii*, which has attained the size of a forest-tree in half a century. Among the flowering trees which made a strong impression by their beauty were the enormous *Magnolia grandiflora* 'Goliath', three specimens, and the exceptionally fine embothriums. Among the shrubs, again, *Fuchsia* in great variety, melaleucas from Australia, *Feijoa sellowiana*, *Mitrairea coccinea* with its pendent tubular flowers of vivid scarlet, and *Berberidopsis corallina*. In one border of the walled garden I first saw watsonias—*beatricis* and *ardenii superba*—doing well and gloriously in flower, and as a result took to growing them myself.

Fota is known among tree-specialists everywhere as an arboretum of fine exotic trees. But whereas the word arboretum suggests a ranged collection, at Fota the trees are planted simply as ornaments to a great park. The conifers are very remarkable, but since I admire rather than know them I must refer the reader to Mr Jenkinson's R.H.S. notes on them. He notes a sixty-foot Himalayan cypress, *Cupressus torulosa corneyana* and a rather taller Californian ally, *C. goveniana;* an East African juniper, *J. procera;* a seventy-foot *Pinus griffithii* from Bhutan and its tender Mexican ally, *P. patula.* These few can be taken as representatives of the Fota policy of planting the best from all over the world excepting the tropics.

One very remarkable tree at Fota is a *Magnolia campbelli* which must be about seventy-five feet tall and which was planted in 1872. I have not seen this Fota one in flower but I am familiar with another, about the same age, in Devon, and this, when it is covered in March with its foot-wide and beautifully substantial flowers is, by a great deal, the most spectacular of the flowering trees which we can grow in the British Isles.

I am not good at the identification of trees and know far too little of the conifers to use their names with assurance. Morever I do not trust the hastily scrawled notes which I took in the course of a tour of Fota during which Mrs Ball named scores of her fine trees for me and told me something of their history. I do recall a big Cork Oak, *Quercus suber* as remarkable for its girth, a "weeping" form of the Swamp Cypress which I had never seen before, and many species of *Cupressus, Chamaecyparis, Tsuga, Picea, Abies, Thuya,* and other American and Asiatic conifers which were all new to me.

I have already mentioned *Drimys aromatica*, with its sweetly pungent leaf scent, as outstandingly good. Specimens of *Drimys winteri* in more than one form are also remarkable. The genera *Podocarpus, Abies, Picea, Tsuga,* and *Cryptomeria* are all represented by their most interesting species, and in almost every case quite exceptionally well-grown, and so is *Nothofagus*, the evergreen 'beech' of the Southern Hemisphere. A complete list of the very remarkable trees at Fota would be tedious for the non-botanical reader, and as for the botanical-gardener and the dendrologist, for him a visit to Fota is necessary, for the quality as well as the variety of trees in this fine park can be equalled in only one other Irish garden, Castlewellan in the North, and perhaps nowhere else in our latitudes.

Fota, the great formal garden in Co. Cork, where masonry and living plants combine to create a whole gallery of garden pictures.

Fota. Trees collected from all five Continents reach their full stature in this remarkable garden on the seashore of Co. Cork.

A feature which is most pleasing, especially for those with romantic tastes in gardening, and which, by reason of its darkness, almost defeated even my friend William MacQuitty with his cameras, is the quite extensive grotto or hermitage of moss- and fern-grown rocks, planted with numerous *Dicksonia* tree-ferns, and all in the dense shade of conifers and hardwoods. I know nothing like it in any other garden anywhere than this piece of eighteenth-century romantic fancy carried out in plants from New Zealand! An attempt, which seemed to be succeeding, was being made when I was there to establish *Cyathea dealbata* with young plants sent from Rossdohan. Another very agreeable feature of the park is the lake, set in fine emerald turf and backed by handsome groups of trees.

The enclosures in the walled and the hedged gardens are, for the most part, lawn surrounded by wide borders. There are some very interesting wall-shrubs and there were, again at the time of my visit, fine hybrid fuchsias, watsonias, agapanthus and other exotics. But, as I have said and, I hope, managed to justify, it is for the park and the trees that one goes to Fota.

8
Ardsallagh and Mount Congreve

ARDSALLAGH

As well as Annes Grove and Fota there are other considerable gardens whose names, at least, are known to many, in this same part of Ireland: the Duke of Devonshire's Lismore, for example, has some fine exotics, but I am not familiar with that garden. In this chapter I shall turn from these to look at one fairly new garden on a rather smaller scale but which is of very remarkable quality; and a great Irish garden in the process of remaking. The latter is Mount Congreve in Co. Waterford; and the former Ardsallagh in Co. Tipperary, is of particular interest for it shows what a brilliant gardener can accomplish in relatively few years, given the soils and climate of southern Ireland; moreover, being on a smaller scale, although still large by average English standards, it is a little more in keeping with modern gardening practice or fashion, imposed by economic conditions rather than taste, than the great woodland gardens we have been dealing with.

This work of modern garden art is near Fethard in Co. Tipperary, and it really is astonishing what has been accomplished by Mrs B. Farquar, its maker, in about fifteen years. For in 1949, when Mrs Farquar bought Ardsallagh, it was simply a farmhouse and farmyard. I am not concerned here with the transformation of the house, which had first priority. Before a garden could be started it was necessary, as is usual in Ireland, to plant a shelter belt of trees and hedges against the prevailing winds off the Atlantic. In this part of the work quick results were achieved by the lifting and replanting of fully-grown trees, mostly conifers; this practice is as old as the eighteenth century, but in our own time it has become an exact science and can be done with confidence that the trees will live if certain rules are observed. It has always been, and still remains, expensive, but it saves years of waiting. At all events, it was not until 1951 that the planting of the garden proper was begun. Yet as early as 1960, when I first saw it, it had a pleasing and convincing look of maturity and, in some genera, the plants were the finest I had seen of their kind.

Mount Congreve in Co. Waterford, where lavish new plantings are extending one of Ireland's greatest romantic gardens.

The principal divisions of Ardsallagh are as follows: a shrub and herbaceous garden on what we may call Robinson-Jekyll lines, that is not a wild garden but one in which the woody and the herbaceous plants are planted together to grow in harmony "after" Nature, the plantations being threaded by meandering walks; a formal garden walled and paved with good flagstone paths, enclosed in fine hedges protecting shrubs and herbaceous perennial borders, and subdivided by clipped hedges, some of them beech, into enclaves; a walled rectangular kitchen garden with espalier fruit trees and a range of greenhouses; a sunk garden with a lily pool and an alpine terrace; and a courtyard garden of outstanding interest. All of these are successful and all are impeccably maintained.

The courtyard garden, immediately by the house, is one of the most charming things of its kind I have ever seen. In the spirit of the Italian, more specifically Tuscan, "Garden room" it is, however, carried out in and furnished not with plants one associates with such secret enclosed gardens, but a very remarkable collection of tender exotics which, by grace of Ireland's mild winters, and of the high stone walls, not only survive but flourish. It should, however, be emphasised that although the exotic nature of the plants used in this courtyard adds much to its interest and quality, what really matters is the success of the design as a whole, aesthetically rather than merely horticulturally.

Planted to the walls are a number of exceptionally interesting climbers: there are two clematis species, both evergreens, *indivisa* and *armandii*, and in both the flowers are borne in large branching racemes or panicles, are very beautifully formed, and are white. The first, of course, is very tender, a New Zealander. Then there is *Mutisia decurrens*, a climbing composite from the Argentine mountains with orange, or in some cases red, daisy flowers of great size and substance. This mutisia is not tender, for it grows wild in the region of, for example, San Carlos de Barriloche, but it is very rare in our gardens. *Mandevilla suaveolens*, Chilean jasmine, has sweetly fragrant flowers as big as the trumpet flowers of our common bindweed. *Jasminum polyanthum*, with its immense branched pinacles of flowers whose buds are red, though they open white, is as fragrant as, and much more floriferous than, the common jasmine; but, again, it is tender — it is killed out of doors in Devon — and so is the New Zealand "Glory Pea", *Clianthus puniceus*, more curious than beautiful, with the proportions of the huge pea-flowers so altered that they look like the claws of a boiled lobster. Among other Australasians in this planting are two very interesting and manage-ably small bottle-brush shrubs: *Acacia verticellata* with needle-like foliage and pale cream flowers, a most attractive species; and *Melaleuca gibbosa* whose flowers are mauve. The ever-green crinodendron and embothrium provide vivid reds in their season. The centre of the courtyard is occupied by a group of three *Eucalyptus*, nicely associated together, *dalrym-pleana*, *coccifera*, and *parviflora*. These have been skilfully managed, cut down to branch low and form spreading rather than mastlike trees.

Mount Congreve. The Maidenhair tree *Gingko biloba* in the herbaceous garden. This magnificent specimen is probably a female plant.

Ardsallagh is on limestone; yet the garden has flourishing rhododendrons, and many of the other plants, including some already named, are calcifuges.

Mrs Farquar has achieved success with these by making raised beds with the peat which is never far to seek in Ireland; by making sure that these are always above the level of the surrounding ground, so that no lime-laden water is leached into them, these beds are kept acid and the lime-hating plants happy.

In the lily pool or sunk garden, with its well-contrived terrace of alpines, the policy has been the same as in the courtyard garden; that is to say, the design is traditional and so is the style of gardening, but a very large number of the plants are tender exotics. Among these are *Myosotidium nobile*, flourishing as I have rarely seen it in our hemisphere, and seeding itself freely; it is given a diet of seaweed, for this is very much a seaside plant and is said, indeed, to do exceptionally well if fed with rotten fish. Among the trees which help to contain this garden I noted well-grown *Eucalyptus viminalis*. One of the most charming of shrubby exotic alpines is *Penstemon roezlii*, with rather round, very glaucous leaves, a prostrate habit and soft maroon-red flower spikes; after seeing it at Ardsallagh I took to growing it in Devon where it does very well and seems quite hardy. Another beautiful ground-covering evergreen shrub of this garden is *Leptospermum prostratum;* the flowers are white. I liked the heath-like *Fabiana imbricata*, and among the young callistemons planted here it was good to see *phoeniceus*, whose bottle-brush flowers are finer than in the less tender species and whose foliage, with the soft coppery-red young shoots, is very superior.

Among the groundlings which are very good in the shrub and herbaceous garden, the genera *Primula* and *Meconopsis* are represented by their best species; and among the shrubs *Robinia kelseyii*, a corokia, and the gaunt but handsome, winter-flowering *Mahonia lomariifolia* are notable. But the shrubs which are really superlative in this garden are *Hydrangea villosa* and *Hydrangea heterophylla*. On one visit to Ardsallagh I saw these at the height of their flowering season, and they were better grown and more floriferous than I have seen them anywhere else even in Ireland, although they are very beautiful also at Birr Castle.

It is difficult to convey in words the qualities of this remarkable young garden; the wide range of plant material, the splendid growth of the plants, the impeccably clean gardening, the taste in design and layout, the solution of the problem of using exotic plants in traditional styles of planting, the successful sustaining of eager expectation and satisfied surprise, these are, no doubt, the chief attributes of its success.

MOUNT CONGREVE

It has not been possible to establish that any particular member of the Congreve family was responsible for the laying out of the gardens and the planting of the very beautiful park, the high terraces and walks above the valley of the River Suir, of Mount Congreve. But it is

New plantings of azaleas and heaths into the woods at Mount Congreve.

very unlikely that any ancestor of the present owner, Mr Ambrose Congreve, can have gardened the place on the scale he has initiated. Perhaps there is no garden in all Europe which is being replanned and replanted on such a scale today, and in another ten or fifteen years the place cannot fail to be a very remarkable spectacle in the months of late spring. It is an exceptionally pleasing and interesting one.

Mount Congreve is near Waterford, and the river Suir flows through its grounds. The Georgian house, now in the process of being gutted and restored and very thoroughly modernised inside, was built by John Congreve in 1725. The most distinguished members of the Congreve family, cousins of the Mount Congreve line, were not gardeners; they were William Congreve, the dramatist; and another William Congreve who invented matches and also the first rocket weapons — his rockets were used by the Royal Navy at the battle of Copenhagen. Mr Congreve writes to me that, ". . . In the eighteenth and nineteenth centuries the family was rather too well off and do not seem to have made much effort to gain distinction." This perhaps was a good thing from our point of view, for the Congreves stayed at home and made a great garden which is, after all, Voltaire's recipe for a contented and useful life.

Mr Ambrose Congreve, true son of his generation, has associated with his garden a very large plant-propagating unit which produces young plants, especially such flowering shrubs as azalea and camellia and many evergreens, for export to Britain and elsewhere. This is a very sensible way of meeting part of the enormous expenses of a great garden. Many of the great horticultural masterpieces of the past have had to be neglected, and have fallen into decay, for want of some such initiative, and a well-stocked old garden is usually a good source of valuable propagating material.

The gardens can be considered in two parts: the woodland garden which is vast and, in some parts more parklike than wood-like, so that walks among the magnificent old trees, with glades planted with azaleas and other flowering shrubs, open into wide vistas of fine turf decorated with specimen trees or groups of trees. And the vast walled garden of lawns, wide and well-planted herbaceous borders, and a good range of greenhouses which must originally have been succession houses. The herbaceous perennials grown in the borders are magnificent, well up to Chelsea Flower Show standards; and while this is not my favourite kind of gardening, it is something to be seen in the height of its season, for it is becoming rare. The walled garden also has superbly grown shrubs, not rarities, the kind we can all grow, but exceptionally well done: they include *Hydrangea villosa*, *H. paniculata* and *H. sargentiana*, the latter almost a small tree; and a whole range of the best *Buddleia davidii* cultivars, the most handsome of these being 'Black Knight'. There are also some fine specimens of the much more delicately beautiful *B. fallowiana* 'Lochinch'. One remarkable ornament of the walled garden is an immense, spreading and shapely *Gingko biloba*.

Mount Congreve. The lawns and herbaceous borders of the walled garden make a semi-
formal nucleus to one of the grandest woodland gardens in Europe. This is one of the very
few Irish gardens in which planting of flowering trees and shrubs still continues on a lavish
scale as Mr. Ambrose Congreve continues the work of his ancestors.

Oriental poppies in the herbaceous border at Mount Congreve.

In the park and woodland gardens Mount Congreve begins with the advantage of a fine, steep fall of land from the house level down to the river. The hillside, traversed by gently graded walks, has some very fine specimen trees, especially cedars and other conifers, but with many good hardwoods too. Planted beside the walks, and into glades in the lower, woodland parts, are flowering shrubs in a really impressive range and in immense numbers. Mr Congreve plants on a lavish scale. Among the more remarkable of the older, or at least well-established shrubs and flowering trees, are tremendous embothriums which produce thousands of seedlings all round them; fine groups of *Clerodendron fargesii* and *C. trichoto-mum;* and, most interesting to compare with the *Embothrium*, its South American ally, the Tasmanian *Telopea truncata*, which I have seen as good only at the Slieve Donard nursery in County Down.

The new plantings, into the glades and beside the broad, high walks, include hundreds of magnolias in all the species in cultivation; such rhododendrons as *sinogrande* and *maca-beanum* not in ones but again in hundreds. I recall, in particular, one group of fifty *R. macabeanum* which will, in years to come, provide one of the most remarkable features in any garden anywhere. All the planting is done in masses, and Mr Congreve is never a "spotty" planter. Perhaps I can give a single instance to exemplify the scale of the work

Even the trees of Mount Congreve are gardened with many species of clematis and other climbing plants.

and the spirit in which it is being done: *Magnolia campbelli*—a large tree when mature, and rare in gardens, for although hardy its early habit exposes its incomparable flowers to March frost—is, when in flower, probably the most spectacular and beautiful of the flowering trees which can be grown in the temperate and sub-tropical zones of the world; its flowers are rose pink, numerous on mature trees, from nine inches to as much as a foot in diameter and of a very beautiful form. Along his River Suir walk at the lower level of the garden Mr Congreve has planted, then, *Magnolia campbelli*. Half a dozen, a dozen, a score? No: eighty. That walk will, in twenty years time, present a spectacle unequalled in its kind anywhere in the world.

I am bound to say that I am less happy about the plantings, up in the woods, of massed embothriums, as many as fifty to a group: the burning scarlet of this Chilean Fire-tree is so overwhelming that it needs discreeter handling, or so it seems to me. On the other hand the planting of azaleas into the woodland glades, of clematis to climb old trees, and the splendid new works in stone and water, are all admirable.

Mount Congreve is already a very grand garden. As a woodland garden, if it be maintained in the spirit of Mr Congreve's planting, it will, in years to come, be one of the glories of Ireland.

9

Powerscourt

The foregoing eight chapters will have given the impression that, Ilnacullin Italianate not-withstanding, the Irish garden is a plantsman's paradise and the garden architect's despair. There is a point of view, and a perfectly valid one, that the plant material used in making a garden is of only secondary importance and that what matters is design and layout. The restricted range of the plants used in the great and the lesser Italian gardens of the Renaissance and pre-Renaissance makes a good demonstration of this point; moreover, the same truth is established by the gardens of Japan. Plantsmanship makes the great gardens of Ireland, as of Britain, extraordinarily interesting; but it is not enough. This chapter and Chapter 10 are, therefore, devoted to two cases of the Irish garden in which formal shape and style are far more important than in any garden we have yet dealt with: Powerscourt; and—beyond question one of the most perfect gardens in Europe—Birr Castle.

Powerscourt is a Georgian mansion in the very grandest style, built on a plateau above the River Dargle in County Wicklow—in the Wicklow Hills which offer some of the prettiest scenery in Western Europe. The house is about fifteen miles from Dublin, so that it is very easy to visit from that lovely city. It was completed in 1770, having been forty years in the building. Within the Powerscourt domain, and about two miles from the house, the River Dargle provides a pleasing spectacle of its own accord—the highest waterfall in all Ireland and the British Isles—398 feet in a sheer ribbon of water against shining black rocks.

The view from what is now the half-mile long and very broad and noble terrace before the south front of the house must always have been so impressive as to influence, if not dominate, the ideas of anyone proposing to lay out a garden on that site. The land falls away sharply to a valley, and then rises again; beyond some foothill country and forming a most pleasing horizon, rises the Sugar Loaf mountain, often presenting itself in that extra-ordinary shade of smoky violet-blue which is peculiar to Irish mountains in the distance and gives all the mountainous parts of Ireland their unique character, a soft and rather melancholy beauty all their own. The sixth Lord Powerscourt decided to create a formal garden beyond the south front of his house, making use of this glorious panorama. Whether this was a concept which he simply talked about and dreamed of, or whether drawings were made at this time—about 1840—is not clear, but certainly the work was not started in the sixth lord's time.

One interesting speculation is possible here: whoever was responsible for the tree planting beyond the formal garden and the lake when they had been made, had the skill and knowledge to draw the distant view right into the garden by the manner in which the trees were chosen and planted. It is possible that this was a mere accident; but it may not have been. The technique of bringing a distant countryside into the garden was first developed by the great landscape gardeners of China. By the time Lord Powerscourt was conceiving his garden, descriptions of the method which involves a careful placing of trees according to the weight and colour of their foliage, so as to create false perspectives, had been published. I have shown elsewhere* that to claim that the English landscape gardeners of the eighteenth century learned the art from the Chinese is absurd because it is chronologically impossible. But it is true that this one part of the art, that of bringing the distant scenery into the garden, was learned from China and was described in English in about 1790. Lord Powerscourt or his architect was well read in landscape gardening, and we can add China to the list of countries whose garden art has influenced that of the Irish.

The sixth Lord Powerscourt died in 1844 and the seventh, his son, began to carry out his father's garden plan in 1855. The work took twenty years to complete. From the grand balustraded terrace at the south front of the house, a magnificent double staircase leads by way of a series of evenly placed lower terraces down to a circular lake with a great Triton fountain. The lake is so perfectly framed in tree plantings that the view, both within and beyond the gardens, is open and yet nicely defined. Each terrace on the descent to the lake has its own fountains or statuary. As in all good garden vistas, this one works both ways, that is to say whether one looks down and across to the Sugar Loaf from the level of the house; or up to the house from the south side of the lake.

Not only is this work of art perfectly satisfying as a whole, but, when one comes to a closer examination, the detail is impeccable. The wrought-iron work of gates and doors, for example, is very fine; iron is such a difficult material to work in that it imposes its own discipline, its own purity of line, so that smith's work does not suffer the decadence of other crafts; but the iron work at Powerscourt is particularly fine. The works decorating the several terraces—statues, fountains, stone vases and urns, sundials—are all excellent in their kind. Only the two winged horses flanking the iron balustrade of the lowest terrace, the one on the lake, strike me as being rather weak: Pegasi should be bolder. Even the

*The English Garden.

Powerscourt, Ireland's greatest formal garden. One of the Pegasus statues.

Powerscourt. A superb use of wrought iron.

Powerscourt. Part of the Japanese garden, which adjoins the formal garden.

The lake at Powerscourt from one of the grottoes, showing the Neptune statue.

patterns formed with cobbles of different shades which pave the stairs and landings are just what they should be, and the detail of the ornaments of the great stone vases ornamenting the balustrades is admirable.

The inspiration of this garden, or rather of this part of the garden, is obvious. I have heard it called 'French', but it is nothing of the kind: anyone who has ever seen such grand Renaissance or Baroque gardens as those of the Villa Aldobrandini, the Villa d'Este, the Villa Doria Pamphili or the Villa Lante can be in no doubt at all that Powerscourt derives from the Renaissance gardens of Rome and its summer resort towns. But there are, of course, great differences: the garden is not contained within a rigid framework of wall but grades off at the sides into woodland, which makes it late Baroque in style; and the manner in which the distant countryside, with the Sugar Loaf mountain central to the view, is brought into the garden, while it obeys the classic Italian rules, (Georgina Masson in her magnificent *Italian Gardens* quotes Alberti as saying that one should have a view of 'familiar mountains' across 'the delicacy of gardens'), is almost Chinese landscape in its perfection.

Before coming to the park-land garden in which the formal garden is set, a word or two about the neighbourhood of the waterfall which belongs to Powerscourt although it is remote from the garden proper. You reach it by walking along a pretty valley planted with trees, and two of the species are of particular interest: the Noble Fir and the Monkey Puzzle. These are planted in considerable numbers. The *Abies nobilis* must have been a rare novelty when planted here; it only reached us from Oregon in 1825. It is the most beautiful of the firs which succeed in Britain, and its cones are magnificent, nine or ten inches long, stout, and in colour a rich purple. As for the Monkey Puzzles, *Araucaria araucana*, the Chilean pine was introduced to Britain in about 1790. It is impossible to judge the beauty of this tree by the specimens in the front gardens of Victorian villas in the suburbs. See it well grown and planted with other trees — there is, for example, a really magnificent specimen at Greenways, Professor and Mrs Mallowan's lovely garden on the River Dart — and its quality is realised. At Powerscourt, in the valley leading to the waterfall, a whole coppice of these araucarias transform part of one side of this valley into something very rich and strange, some of the trees bearing the enormous, corpulent cones which surely inspired the stone ones which top so many stone garden pillars and piers of this period.

The informal gardens about the formal centre of Powerscourt consist of walks among trees, leading to other features of the garden. Of these the only one which does not seem to me entirely successful is the "Japanese" garden made in what was a boggy hollow, by the then Lord Powerscourt, in 1908. I do not, in fact, see what, apart from a good stone lantern which is typical of Japanese garden decoration of one period, is Japanese about it. It is true that such dwarfish conifers as *Tsuga dumosa* and *Picea nigra*, more or less in the Japanese taste, are planted here. On the other hand so are *Callistemon citrinus* which, although interesting and pretty, in flower, are hardly Japanese.

A straight and narrow valley leads north out of the Japanese garden with, on one side, a steep hill planted to some of the finer species and cultivars of rhododendron, and topped by an old castle keep. The feature is a very pleasant one; from three sides of the hill one has a dozen different and pleasing views of the gardens, house and surrounding country. The sides of the south-to-north valley are planted with a collection of exotic conifers which are doing very well indeed; the planting is rather open, as in parkland, than dense as in woodland, thus making possible the interplanting of good rhododendrons, several species of magnolia, and some unusual exotic evergreens. At least two of the evergreens at Powerscourt, the *Photinia davidsonii* in this part of the gardens, and the *Euonymus fimbriata* in another which we shall come to presently, are very rare in gardens; I know of only one other specimen of this euonymus, remarkable for its carmine young growth in spring and its turning brilliant butter yellow later in the year, and that is at Overbeck's in Devon. Some Cornish gardens grow it.

Like all great Irish gardens Powerscourt has its big, square, walled garden, originally for the production of vegetables and cut flowers. It was not of great interest on either of

Powerscourt from the high terrace across the lake to the Sugar Loaf Mountain.

The formal garden at Powerscourt shows both Italian and French Renaissance influences.

my prolonged visits to the garden, although there are some good herbaceous perennials. You reach the walled garden by walking west along the south terrace. And by going into it at one side and out at the far side, you come to a second piece of water-gardening, a formal circular basin called the Green Pond; it is here that one finds the big *Euonymus fimbriata* and, going beyond that, arrives at a stretch of fine open park, turf planted with well-grown specimen trees, the fall of land being, as everywhere at Powerscourt, itself one of the pleasures of the eye. Among the trees are a towering *Picea sitchensis* topping two hundred feet, a very pretty young silver cypress, *Cupressus arizonica fastigiata*, which is so beautifully silvery in Tuscany and so much less so in Ireland and Britain; a *Eucalyptus gunnii* which has attained 120 feet, and a very lovely silver fir, *Abies polita* which, although not old, must be sixty feet tall. Still more interesting in this area of the garden are the southern hemisphere beeches which do so remarkably well in Irish gardens: I know very little about these, but *Notofagus dombeyi* is one; and the flourishing and shapely specimen of *Nothofagus betuloides* is said to be the biggest in Europe at something under fifty feet.

Whether one spends one's time gazing at the score of perfectly satisfying spectacles afforded by the formal garden, moving slowly down one side of the stairway and round the lake and so up the other side; or whether in walking at random in woodland and park, Powerscourt is one of the most impressive gardens I am familiar with, and one of the most pleasing. Its formal centre is a perfect work of art in the manner of the great Renaissance gardens of Italy and France. And its woodland and parkland gardens are full of pleasures for those who favour gardening after nature.

10

Birr Castle

The gardens of Birr Castle are among the best in Europe. They are the creation of the Earl and Countess of Rosse, for although much planting was done before their time, it was for the most part in the park rather than the gardens proper; and even many of the park trees have been planted by the present Lord Rosse. Lady Rosse could hardly have had an upbringing more apt to produce a great gardener: a Messel, her girlhood home — and still her home when she is in Britain — was Nymans in Sussex where her father, the late Colonel Messel, created one of the most remarkable gardens in the world. When Lady Rosse and her husband were planting Birr they received many fine plants from Nymans. Lord Rosse is not only a very good gardener with a wide and deep knowledge of plants; he is a dendrologist of distinction whose collection of exotic trees is world famous among specialists.

Birr is at the very heart of Ireland in County Offaly. This part of Ireland is relatively flat, and in other respects it differs from most of the regions in which the best Irish gardens are to be found. In the first place the climate is not quite so mild, the January Mean Minimum temperature being lower, and severe frosts not uncommon. At a shade over thirty-three inches, the mean annual rainfall is lower than elsewhere in Ireland; on the other hand, there is rather more sunshine. Most of the good Irish gardens are on acid, often very peaty, soils; the soil of Birr Castle gardens is alkaline, which means that for the most part the calcifuge plants will not grow there, although as a matter of fact one species of rhododendron does, as we shall see, flourish. This alkaline soil is, however, very fertile, most of it a deep alluvial loam.

The house, or rather castle, was built in the seventeenth century on the foundations of a mediaeval fortress. But the site was very anciently inhabited: it seems that Saint Brendan, a disciple of Saint Patrick, had his hermitage there, and his Well is still a feature of the grounds. Although the fall of land from the nobly sited house down to the large lake, which was made in the eighteenth century, is gentle, the gardens do not give the impression of

Birr Castle, where the Earl and Countess of Rosse have created one of Ireland's most beautiful gardens.

flatness, in part because the River Camcor, which is the main axis of the garden, flows between relatively steep banks, so that one is not continuously on a single level. And in part because the landscaping and the tree planting have been done with such skill that the gardens are, from the point of view of design, full of incident and movement.

As I have said, although many of the trees, the lake, the walled kitchen garden, were all there before the present Earl of Rosse and Lady Rosse began to garden at Birr, they really are the makers of the garden. Lord Rosse's father was not a gardener but a brilliant and very successful engineer. Among his achievements was the making, largely with his own hands, of the largest telescope in the world at that time — the large masonry chassis of this instrument and part of the tube are still in the grounds, though the lens is at the Science Museum; and the invention of the turbine engine which subsequently powered the Royal Navy's *Dreadnoughts* early in this century. He cannot have had much time for gardening, and so it is that the gardens as we now see them are the creation not of several generations like those of Mount Usher, or even of a century like those of Powerscourt, but of only about twenty-five years. The spectacle of such a garden looking thoroughly mature is always encouraging, for it shows what can be done well within a single lifetime.

The principal divisions of the garden are four in number. First, the lawns, courts and borders in the immediate vicinity of the house, including the walls which are planted with interesting and tender climbers. Secondly, the river garden, that is the gardened parts of the river banks and the land beyond the immediate banks. Then the formal gardens, perhaps the best which have been made in our time and in which a very ancient style is revived. And finally the woodland walks. I do not here include the park, nor the walled kitchen garden and propagating houses. All parts of the gardens are remarkably well "done".

THE FORMAL GARDENS

There are two formal gardens at Birr. First, the Knot Garden of clipped box and pleached arches of hornbeam is in the seventeenth-century manner, the layout being rectangular, of course, and the straight walks terminated by statuary. Here is grown a very good collection of shrub roses, a few of them botanical species but for the most part the "old-fashioned" hybrid roses.

In the second formal garden the knots are of clipped box and shaped turf of fine grass. A main, straight walk is crossed at right angles by transverse walks, all the paths being of fine limestone chips. The crossing points are ornamented by handsome urns on pedestals. It is difficult to over-emphasise the charm of this work. To sit there in the sun, half drunk on the scent of box which always evokes, for me, the great gardens of Queluz north of Lisbon, undistracted by too much colour or by a display of exotic plants, is to be reminded of the merits of that kind of gardening in which design and form are everything, and plantsman-

Birr Castle is outstanding for the happy combinations of formal style with fine plantsmanship.

ship is not important. The principal vista through this garden is completed by fine Irish yews and backed by tall trees.

The formal gardens are linked to an area of flower garden and to the region of the walled kitchen garden and greenhouses by one of the most remarkable features in any Irish, or for that matter British, garden; this is a narrow walk between box hedges, clipped, two centuries old, and about thirty-five feet tall. To the best of my knowledge, this is unique.

THE RIVER GARDEN

The river garden consists of, on one side, a walk beside and above the water, between gardened banks and dominated by a higher walk beyond which is an area of lawns and borders, of shrubs and perennials, and group or clump plantings, opening into part of the park away to the right. (The river, as you walk away from the house, is on your left.) And, on the other bank, walks meandering among trees, shrubs, perennials and bulbous plants, everything being well grown and beautifully associated together, and the style more or less "Robinsonian". The river is crossed by a stone bridge which links the left and right banks. It is remarkable how many good Irish gardens are focused on a river and how well the Irish gardeners have developed the art of planting river banks successfully: Mount Usher, Annes Grove, Mount Congreve, and Birr Castle all owe much of their charm to their rivers.

Now a little about some of the Birr Castle plants. The garden is rich in fine primulas; in mecanopsis, including some of the blue poppies and a remarkable pink one with golden buds. Lilies do well and seem almost to be naturalised in some parts of the gardens: one admirable feature is the regularly spaced tubs along the highest walk above the river, planted with *Lilium speciosum*. Among shrubs, the nature of the soil has led the Rosses to concentrate on calciole species and the collections of *Syringa* and of *Philadelphus* are remarkable. Because of the soil, Birr differs from most Irish gardens in not being a rhododendron garden. However, there is one exception to this rule: *Rhododendron yunnanense*, in several large groups, flourishes splendidly at Birr, a point which other gardeners on alkaline soils might like to note. Lord Rosse told me that this species does perfectly well anywhere on the Birr limestones. One cannot, probably, carry this too far: *R. yunnanense* would not grow in chalk. But it will certainly grow where hundreds of other species of its kind will not. Another interesting phenomenon in this connection is the state and growth of *Eucryphia nymansensis*. This is known to be lime-tolerant, and to inherit this attribute from its *E. cordifolia* parent, for the other parent, *E. glutinosa*, is a lime-hater. At Birr *E. nymansensis* grows and flowers quite well, but it is not, as Lady Rosse pointed out to me, as fine and full as it is on the acid soil of Nymans.

The informal romantic garden at Birr is focused on the river. Rivers are features of many great Irish gardens.

Still among the shrubs, the gardens are remarkable for mahonias, notably *lomariifolia*, *bealii* and *acanthifolia*. *Olearea virgata* and *Meliosma cuneifolia* are very good. At intervals along the river garden are specimens of *Hydrangea villosa* of a great size, carefully pruned to prevent leginess, and almost as fine as those at Ardsallagh. An *Euonymus elatus* is so remarkable for its colour in the autumn that a visiting Chinese specialist remarked that "he had not known that colour to exist outside China".

The courts and terraces about the castle itself are very beautifully gardened and their plant material is of interest. On the walls of the castle itself there are some enormous climbing plants: in his excellent account of these gardens (R.H.S. *Journal* Nov. & Dec. 1964), Mr Lanning Roper made a point about them which demonstrated the taste which governs the whole of the Birr Castle gardens;

> "One of the most striking bits of planting is the exuberant curtain of *Clematis spooneri*, a mauve wisteria and a huge old double Banksian rose, which drape the balustrade of the staircase and clamber to the crenellations three storeys above ground. For all the seemingly careless abandon, these climbers are pruned in winter, tied in and controlled to prevent a too-heavy and overgrown effect about the windows, and to ensure the maximum of bloom. The combination of colours is a happy one, as the clear butter-yellow of the great clusters of small, neatly double roses, the dusty pink of the clematis and the lavender-blue racemes of wisteria are all about the same colour value and have the ideal foil in the grey stone."

Climbers are not the only plants to benefit from the walls. Among others I was struck by a fine tree of kowhai, the *Sophora tetraptera* of New Zealand and a fifteen-foot plant of *Calicarpa giraldiana*.

Like all good gardeners the Rosses avoid spottiness by planting in masses; for example, the daffodils in millions which are a feature of the park in spring are all of one kind. And it is in the same spirit that the courts about the castle, beside the drive on the left of the castle as you approach from the main gates of the park, are planted with a superior species of Blue-eyed Mary, *Omphalodes cappadocica*. This has the same vividly sky-blue flowers as *O. verna*, but in racemes, which are taller and which colour the whole area; the only shrubs here are all the scarlet-crimson flowered chaenomeles, in bloom at the same time as the omphalodes.

On the south-west side of the castle there are wide borders against the castle walls, served by a stone-paved terrace walk connected to the ground floor of the house by a stone stairway. These very sheltered walls and borders are used for tender plants and shrubs.

The courtyards and purlieus
of the Castle at Birr are
richly and skilfully planted.

There is a good *Buddleia auriculata*, a South African species with fragrant, cream flowers; a New Zealand Glory Pea—*Clianthus puniceus* which always fascinates clever gardeners although it seems to me a very ugly plant, at least in cultivation; a very large *Pittosporum tobira*, whose flowers are scented sweetly; a *Carpentaria californica*, an *Indigofera pendula*, and some other exotics.

On the sunny side of the castle, contained between gently sloping grass banks and grassed terraces, there is a formal rose garden. On the shady, north side a good use has been made of the old, deep castle moat which had not been filled in when, in the second half of the eighteenth century the then owner, Sir William Parsons, laid out the park and made the lake. Lord and Lady Rosse had it filled in, using peat and leaf mould to make the deep top soil, and so provided an area of acid soil for the planting of azaleas and some other rhododendrons, camellias, embothriums, and some heathers, with grouped underplantings of lilies and spring-flowering bulbs. Another part of the old moat has been used to make a herbaceous border to bring some of the summer colour near to the house. The wall behind this has two remarkable plants: a specimen of the giant leaved and glaucous night-flowering *Magnolia delavayi* and a big shrub of *Ceanothus impressus*.

One of the charming features which surround the house, on the right-hand grass terrace, is a fifty-five-year old specimen of perfectly regular shape of *Prunus yedonensis* which has flowers of a very faint pink fading to white as they age, underplanted with hundreds of a small, sky-blue scylla. Across from this the left-hand terrace in full sun is planted with *Cytissus*, *Genista*, *Potentilla*, *Buddleia* and *Cistus*.

The principal divisions of Birr Castle gardens are so subdivided into smaller, enclosed gardens that it is difficult to bring them all into this account and, above all, into focus. Beyond the two formal gardens already mentioned and in the region of the greenhouses, frameyards, propagating beds and nursery, there is, for example, this one, described by Mr Lanning Roper in his R.H.S. account already quoted:

"Another small garden of unusual interest lies behind the greenhouses on the axis of the frameyards and one of the hornbeam alleys. Perfectly clipped eight foot yew hedges, with just the right taper to prevent snow-damage, frame a planting of extreme simplicity but exceptional effectiveness. This has four willow-leaved pears (*Pyrus salicifolia pendula*) in the corners and, in the centre a tall pyramidal *Malus tschonoskii*. The pyramidal shape of the malus, its bright pink-red flowers in May and gleaming scarlet autumn foliage form a striking contrast to the broad, rounded and pendulous habit and silvery grey leaves of the pears, all effectively silhouetted against the inky green of the yews."

The castle walls at Birr embellished by climbing plants both familiar and rare.

The park which surrounds the gardens proper is, like all parks, indescribable; words cannot really convey very much about great expanses of grass and trees. But because it is of such importance as an arboretum I have appended a list of the trees to be seen in it.

CONIFERS

Tree	Year Planted
Abies:	
alba	before 1860
balsamea	1921
cephalonica	before 1860
cephalonica apollinis	1929
chensiensis	1945
cilicica	1937
faxoniana	1933
firma	1930
forrestii	1942
fraseri	1921
gamblei	1947
georgei	1945
grandis	1908
holophylla	1927
homolepis	1921
kawakamii	1929
lowiana	1925
nordmanniana	before 1860
numidica	1933
pinsapo var. *glauca*	1927
recurvata	1916
squamata	1930
sutchuenensis	1933
veitchii	1945
Cedrus:	
atlantica	before 1860
atlantica glauca	1921
libani	1930
Cephalotaxus:	
drupacea	1926
fortunei	1934
Cryptomeria:	
japonica	C. 1912
japonica elegans	before 1900
Cupressus:	
arizonica	1927
formosensis	1934
guadalupensis	C. 1912
lawsoniana	before 1860
lawsoniana fraseri	1926

Tree	Year Planted
Cupressus:	
lawsoniana 'Triomphe de Boskoop'	1927
lawsoniana westermannii	1931
lawsoniana youngii	1931
lusitanica	before 1860
lusitanica benthamii	1930
macnabiana	1933
macrocarpa	before 1860
macrocarpa lutea	1926
nootkatensis	before 1860
sempervirens	1927
thyoides	1933
torulosa	1927
Larix occidentalis	C. 1912
Libocedrus chilensis	1933
Gingko biloba	1946
Juniperus:	
chinensis	before 1900
communis succica	1942
coxii	1946
formosana	1946
recurva (base)	before 1860
rigida	1942
squamata	1946
squamata meyeri	1946
Metasequoia glyptostra bodies	1953
Picea:	
asperata	1916
bicolor	1933
brachytyla	1927
engelmanii	1925
glauca	1925
jezoensis	1921
koyamai	1927
likiangensis	1916
maximowiczii	1929
morrisonicola	1929
omorika	1921
omorika pendula	1931
orientalis	1860
polita	1929
pungens	1916

Birr Castle gardens make very clever use of the fall of land. The plants in tubs are *Lilium speciosum* and *Agapanthus*.

Tree	Year Planted		Tree	Year Planted
Picea:			*Podocarpus:*	
purpurea	1916		*andinus*	1930
rubra	1930		*totara*	1938
smithiana	1921		*Pseudotsuga:*	
spinulosa	1929		*taxifolia*	before 1860
wilsonii	1916		*taxifolia*	1908
Pinus:			*Sequoia gigantea*	before 1860
armandii	1947		*Taxodium distichum*	C. 1912
ayacahuite	1946		*Taxus media hicksii*	1946
contorta latifolia	1927		*Thuja:*	
holfordiana	1938		*orientalis*	1947
leucodermis	1927		*plicata*	before 1900
monticola	1929		*standishii*	1934
muricata	1927		*Torreya:*	
pinaster	1921		*californica*	1921
pinea	1929		*grandis*	1921
radiata	1911		*nucifera*	1937
rigida	1927		*Tsuga:*	
strobus	C. 1912		*caroliniana*	1934
tabuliformis	1944		*chinensis*	1951
thunbergii	1927		*heterophylla*	1921
wallichiana	before 1900		*sieboldii*	1934

MAPLES

Tree	Year Planted		Tree	Year Planted
Acer:			*Acer:*	
argutum	1938		*henryi*	1930
barbinerve	1933		*hersii*	1933
buergerianum	1931		*hyrcanum*	1933
cappadocicum	C. 1912		*japonicum nitifolium*	1949
circinatum	1927		*laxiflorum*	1935
cissifolium	1930		*leucoderme*	1953
davidii	1943		*lobelii*	1932
diabolicum	1938		*macrophyllum*	1942
fargesii	1953		*mandshuricum*	1932
franchetii	1931		*maximowiczii*	1932
ginnala	1927		*monspessulanum*	1933
ginnala aidzuense	1941		*neglectum*	1933
griseum	C. 1912		*neglectum elongatum*	1933
grosseri	1932		*nikoënse*	C. 1916
heldreichii	1934		*oliverianum*	1942

Birr. A glimpse of the lakeside.

A corner of one of the walled gardens.

Tree	Year Planted
Acer:	
opalus	1935
opalus obtusatum	1932
palmatum	C. 1912
palmatum 'Atropurpureum'	C. 1916
palmatum 'Involutum'	1931
palmatum 'Koreanum'	1939
palmatum 'Osakazuki'	1929
palmatum 'Septemlobum' (base)	C. 1912
palmatum 'Shishigashira'	1929
pennsylvanicum	1953
pentaponicum	1932
pictum mono	1938
platanoides dissectum	C. 1912
platanoides schwedleri	C. 1912
pseudoplatanus brilliantissimum	C. 1916

Tree	Year Planted
Acer:	
pseudoplatanus purpureum	C. 1912
purpurascens	1933
rotundilobum	1932
rubripes	1942
rubrum	C. 1912
rubrum tomentosum	1938
rufinerve	1929
saccharinum	C. 1912
saccharum	1937
sieboldianum	1953
spicatum	1937
tataricum	1932
tetramerum betulifolium	1932
trautvetteri	1932
triflorum	1933
truncatum	1938
ukurunduense	1951

MAGNOLIAS

Magnolia:	
acuminata	1930
campbellii	1946
dawsoniana	1946
delavayi	1916
grandiflora 'Goliath'	1929
kobus	1931
loebneri	1949
mollicomata	1946
officinalis	1942
sargentiana	1938
sargentiana robusta	1949
sieboldii	1951
sinensis	1946
soulangeana alexandrina	1938
soulangeana rustica rubra	1938
sprengeri 'Diva'	1953
sprengeri elongata	1950
stellata	C. 1912

Magnolia:	
thompsoniana	1939
veitchii	1934
wilsonii	1939
Aesculus:	
carnea	before 1900
indica	1930
neglecta	1933
neglecta prythroblascos	1939
parviflora	C. 1912
turbinata	1933
Ailanthus altissima	before 1900
Alnus:	
cordata	1929
glutinosa laciniata	1946
hirsuta	1931
incana	1929

Birr Castle, from one of the riverside walks. The Earl and Countess of Rosse have here created both formal and wild gardens of outstanding beauty.

Tree	Year Planted		Tree	Year Planted
Alnus:			**Fagus:**	
japonica	1931		sylvatica rotundifolia	1938
subcordata	1929		sylvatica zlatia	1953
			Fraxinus:	
Betula:			americana	1929
albo-sinensis	1934		angustifolia lentiscifolia	1929
ermani	1934		dimorpha	1950
jacquemontii	1937		excelsior aurea	1929
papyrifera	1946		excelsior heterophylla	before 1860
utilis	1934		lanceolata	1927
			longicuspis sieboldiana	1929
Buxus sempervirens	before 1800		mariesii	1929
Carpinus:			paxiana	1929
caroliniana	1934		pennsylvanica aucubaefolia	1929
japonica	1934		rhynchophylla	1937
turczaninovii	1943		spaethiana	1929
			velutiana	1929
Carrierea calycina	C. 1916			
Carya:			**Gleditschia triacanthos**	C. 1916
cordiformis	1934		**Juglans:**	
laciniosa	1934		cathayensis	1941
tomentosa	1934		nigra	1935
			sieboldiana	1941
Catalpa:			vilmoriniana	1930
bignonioides	1930			
bungei	1930		**Liquidambar:**	
fargesii	1931		formosana monticola	1934
speciosa	1930		styraciflua	1921
Cedrela sinensis	1930		**Lirioendron:**	
Celtis occidentalis	1937		chinense	1938
Cercidiphyllum:			tulipifera	1911
japonicum	C. 1912		tulipifera fastigiata	1929
sinense	1939			
			Meliosma cuneifolia	C. 1916
Cercis siliquastrum	1942		**Nothofagus:**	
Corylus colurna	1936		cunninghami	1943
Davidia involucrata	C. 1912		dombeyi	1932
Ehretia dicksoni	1934		obliqua	1934
Eucommia ulmoides	1929		procera	1934
Eucryphia nymansensis	1934			
			Paulownia imperialis	1916
Fagus:			**Phellodendron lavallei**	1951
engleriana	1927		**Platanus:**	
orientalis	1950		acerifolia	before 1860
sieboldii	1927		cuneata	1938
sylvatica fastigiata	1933		orientalis insularis	1935
sylvatica pendula	1933		orientalis laciniata	1937
sylvatica rohanii	1953			

Tree	Year Planted	Tree	Year Planted
Platanus:		*Salix:*	
parviloba	1937	*magnifica*	1927
		vitellina britzensis	1927
Populus:		*Sophora japonica*	1943
canescens	before 1900	*Sorbus:*	
grandidentata	1927	*aria lutescens*	1930
lasiocarpa	1927	*aria majestica*	1930
maximowiczii	1927	*discolor*	1933
nigra var. *italica*	C. 1912	*domestica*	1933
trichocarpa	C. 1925	*pinnatafida gibbsii*	1933
yunnanensis	1927	*scalaris*	1937
		serotina	1939
Pterocarya:		*torminalis*	1933
fraxinifolia	(base) 1930	*vestita*	1939
rehderiana	1932	*yunnanensis*	1951
rhoifolia	1937		
stenoptera	(base) 1937	*Tilia:*	
		americana	1930
Quercus:		*chingiana*	1946
alpestris	1941	*dasystyla*	C. 1912
castaneifolia	1934	*euchlora*	1930
cerris	1934	*henryana*	1946
coccinea	1929	*miqueliana*	1937
conferta	1934	*moltkei*	C. 1912
glabrescens	1945	*petiolaris*	1930
imbricaria	1931	*platyphyllos*	
laurifolia darlingtonii	1934	*asplenifolia*	before 1900
lucombeana	before 1860	*Ulmus:*	
lucombeana fulhamensis	1930	*alata*	1933
lusitanica	1933	*carpinifolia*	1937
macedonica (trojana)	1934	*fulva*	1930
macranthera	1934	*glabra fastigiata*	1937
mirbeckii (canariensis)	1931	*glabra fastigiata aurea*	1937
pedunculata fastigiata	1933	*procera* 'Louis van	
rubra	1946	Houtte'	1937
suber	C. 1912	*procera purpurascens*	1937
toza	1934	*pumila*	1937
turneri	1929	*pumila pinnato-ramosa*	1937
variabilis	1934	*serotina*	1952
wislizenii	1939	*stricta*	1937
		vegeta	1930
Rhus cotinoides	C. 1912	*viminalis*	1937
Robinia:		*viminalis aurea*	1937
kelseyi	1930		
pseudacacia	before 1900	*Zelkova:*	
		carpinifolia	1934
Salix:		*serrata*	C. 1916
coerulea	1927	*sinica*	1934

11

Rowallane

Rowallane is a garden set in the gentle hills of County Down. It is six miles inland, Strangford Loch being the nearest point to the sea, and three hundred feet above sea level. Saintfield is the nearest village, twelve miles from Belfast. The garden is fairly well protected by the shape of the land and by tree plantings from the wind, and although the actual rainfall is low for Ireland, about thirty-six inches, the air is always humid. The soil is light and shallow, and although there are frosts in the winter they are rarely severe.

The garden is not an old one. Its maker, Mr Armitage Moore, inherited the property in 1903, and started to plant in that year although he did not live in the house until 1917. He was a skilful gardener not only in the sense of being a good plantsman who raised many of the trees and shrubs he needed from seed, but as a designer who knew how to make good use of the lie and fall of the land he had to plant. (In 1952 he was awarded the highest honour which the Royal Horticultural Society has in its gift, the Victoria Medal of Honour.)

During and after the Second World War, rising prices, shortage of labour and a falling income forced the owners and makers of Rowallane to let parts of the garden go and to concentrate on the rest, and even then, with only two men instead of six, it was very difficult to keep so considerable an area in order. The pleasure grounds were allowed to go rather wild, the rock garden and the Bishop's rock garden were abandoned. This was a matter of concern not only to garden enthusiasts all over the world, but to the public as well, for the garden had always been open to and had been visited annually by thousands of visitors. As a result of negotiations initiated by the then President of the Royal Horticultural Society, the National Trust, with a grant from the Government of Northern Ireland, assumed responsibility for the garden and set about restoring it to what it was at its zenith in Mr Armitage Moore's time.

Like most good gardens of its type, Rowallane is much divided into enclosures. The first of these, on one's left as one stands facing the front of the house, is the wall garden, and

Rowallane. Rhododendrons and azaleas planted into the natural scene make an astonishing spring spectacle in this Northern Irish garden.

its layout is formal and geometrical, with straight paths crossing at right angles, enclosing rectangular beds and borders. These are planted with both shrubs and herbaceous perennials, as well as many bulbous plants, notably the immense *Cardiocrinum giganteum*. Among the best of the perennials are primulas in variety, mecanopsis in variety, rodgersias. It is one of the distinctions of Rowallane that many of its plants, in several families, are named for the garden, having originated there as garden plants: the best known of these is probably *Hypericum* x 'Rowallane', by the far the finest of the St. John's Worts, although unfortunately not hardy in the average climate of Britain. It can be seen, with its great golden cups of flowers, in most Irish gardens but in England is confined to the warmer counties. Other Rowallane plants—both these examples are to be found in the wall garden—are *Primula* x 'Rowallane Rose' and the magnificent *Viburnum tomentosum* 'Rowallane'.

Among the most interesting flowering trees and shrubs of the wall garden, the group of *Magnolia wilsoni* and *watsoni* with hanging saucer-shaped flowers, the pink-flowered *Magnolia veitchii*, an *Abutilon vitifolium* and a fine *Camellia reticulata* are all outstanding. The walls, of course, are used for tender climbers, among these *Berberidopsis corallina* and *Schizandra rubiflora* being the most attractive, although much rarer are *Clemataclethra lasioclada* and *Trachelospermum jasminoides*.

This wall garden is interesting at almost any time of year, but at its best in late spring and early autumn, the latter season being glorified by the flowering of the later hoherias, although some of these flower in July.

Opening out of the wall garden is a smaller enclosure, a right-angled triangle with a concave hypotenuse, called the outer wall garden. The layout continues to be formal but the planting is not and this small garden is described by the National Trust Guide to the garden as follows.

"Here, according to the time of the year, can be seen the hanging racemes of an ancient wistaria, species roses, nerines or watsonias. *Actinidia kolomikta* can be found against the wall close to *Azara lanceolata* and *Myrtus leitchlinii*, rounding the corner a great tree of *Davidia involucrata*, the 'Handkerchief Tree', towers overhead. A large tree of *Magnolia dawsoniana* flowers and fruits freely. *Eucryphias* 'Nymansay', *moorei* and *lucida* grow beside the Chilean Firebush, *Embothrium lanceolatum*. In the autumn the colchicums which grow under *Hydrangea villosa* flower at the same time, they are grown in variety. Amongst the species *Hydrangea* the visitor should not overlook *H. sargentiana*, an immense plant which has seeded itself in crevices in the wall above. There are some good plants of the Exbury hybrid rhododendrons, 'Lady Chamberlain', 'Lady Roseberry' and 'Lady Berry'.

One of the vistas through the wild garden at Rowallane.

More lilies and meconopsis. Near by is a plant of *Rheum alexandrea* close to a big group of *Euphorbia sikkimensis* and a young tree of *Sorbus sargentiana* with *Cladrastis sinensis* beyond, and near the greenhouse *Hypericum* 'Rowallane Hybrid' raised in this garden. Now we must leave this part of the garden by the iron gate, noticing on the left as we go *Adenocarpus bacqui*. Then cross a bit of rough ground where there is a handsome tree of *Populus maximowiczii* whose long catkins in June turn to fluffy rolls of cotton wool at seed time; a gate then brings us into the Spring Garden."

One of the most successful wild garden plantings in Ireland, although it is possible to criticise it on the grounds that in May the masses of colour, against the soft and gentle coloration of the Irish countryside, are too overwhelming, the spring garden is an expanse of hilly, undulating short turf with some rocky outcrops, and into this have been planted, as dense boskage threaded by narrow paths, masses of azaleas and other rhododendrons. The plantings are well done, of course, with a broad vista through the centre and fine trees to back them, and to most visitors the startling masses of colour are as attractive as they are spectacular. Although this part of Rowallane is called the spring garden, its merits are not confined to that season, for plantings of such autumn colour shrubs as enkianthus and fothergilla make it very brilliant again in the autumn.

South beyond the spring garden is the rock garden, which is rapidly recovering from neglect and where primulas, mecanopsis and many other genera, including some of the very dwarf rhododendrons, have a perfect foil in the rocky outcrops. Also beyond the spring garden lies an enclosure called new ground remarkable for some very fine rhododendrons, for hydrangeas which are more vividly blue here than in most soils, eurcryphias and lomatias. The maples here make a fine glow of colours late in the season.

One of the most successful examples of "Robinsonian" gardening, the planting of exotics into a natural scene, lies to the east of the above enclosures and is called the old wood. The original scene is one of large slabs of granite outcropping through fine turf, a small stream, and some Scots pines. Into this were planted daffodils, including many dwarfs which flower in March, rhododendrons, heathers, camellias and some water plants beside the stream, notably fine rodgersias, and that very striking and, to my taste, grotesque, plant *Lysichitum*, the huge aroid which the Americans call Skunk Cabbage.

This old wood garden contains one of the best collections of the better rhododendron species in the world, and it includes such tender species as *griffithianum, fragrantissimum* and others of the series which have huge, white, scented flowers and far more distinction than most of the rest. Also well represented are *Pieris* and *Drimys*, including *D. colorata*, perhaps the most colourful foliage plant which can be grown in Ireland.

Rowallane. Both rare and familiar herbaceous perennials are planted among small shrubs in a style which is becoming general.

For the next two enclosures on a wandering way back, in a circle, towards the house, I shall quote again from the National Trust Guide:

HOSPITAL

"It was to the 'Hospital' that the sick calves were brought in the days when Rowallane was a farm because it was, and still is, so well sheltered from the icy winds, and here the calves throve as do the half-hardy plants now. The *Drimys winterii* is proof of this, or the *Desfontainea spinosa*, which is an immense bush now. The witch-hazel, *Hamamelis mollis*, was transplanted when quite a big plant from the gardens of the late Sir John Ross of Bladensburg at Rostrevor. Here again we find the 'Handkerchief' tree, and if it is seen with its white bracts hanging it is not hard to understand how it came by its name. *Decaisnea fargesi* grows beside one of the paths leading out of the old wood and, can be recognised in the autumn by the blue pods which hang from the twigs like mice strung up to dry. Of the *Viburnums*, *V. tomentosum var. plicatum* makes a good display and *V. hupehense* produces its scarlet fruit in the autumn when *Disanthus cercidifolias'* turns crimson. The pieris are lovely in the spring with their Lily of the Valley flowers and scarlet young foliage. There are fine specimens of *Nothofagus*, *Acer* and *Eucryphia* as well as *Stewartia* and *Styrax*. Attention might be drawn to the various specimens of *Athrotaxis*, *Podocarpus*, *Cupressus* and *Libocedrus* before we make a slight detour to the

STREAM GROUND

where in May the big bank of *triflorum* rhododendrons will be in flower. If we investigate a small path that scrambles over the rock we shall find plants of *Viburnum carlesii*, *Osmanthus delavayii* growing close to *Corylopsis pauciflora* and *Magnolia salicifolia* with self-sown seedling *Leptospermum* near by. This will take us back into the 'Hospital'. The left hand path leads back past the Half Circle which is beautiful in spring and autumn with azaleas, fothergillas and enkianthus, to the top of the spring garden, but following the lower path out of the 'Hospital' we pass a magnificent specimen of the Chilean Firebush, *Embothrium longifolium*, shown up so well by *Cupressus obtusa var. crippsii* near to *Pistacia sinensis* and so past the Holly Rock with its azaleas on the right, and on the left a group of *Azalea elbrechtii* with *Kolkwitzia amabilis*, and before reaching the Paddock we pass *Cornus kousa* and *Cornus florida rubra* with two groups of rhododendrons on either hand, *Cladrastis sinensis*, *Osmanthus forrestii*, various *Sorbus* and *Cotoneaster*. . . ."

The gardens proper are set in parkland which is divided up into a number of plantings

Part of the rock garden at Rowallane, which is one of the most richly planted in Europe.

Rowallane. Facing the main azalea planting is a magnificent specimen of the Handkerchief tree, *Davidia involucrata*.

—the Pleasure Grounds, the Home Wood, the Paddock and so forth, whose principal beauty and interest consists in fine specimen trees and splendid vistas. However, there are also many interesting shrubs and flowering trees which can properly be considered "garden plants". For example, in the Paddock, remarkable for a collection of nothofagus species which attract the admiration and attention of tree-lovers, there are maples, crabs, flowering plums and cherries and some fine viburnums. Also a gigantic Musk Rose, *Rosa moschata grandiflora*, which has grown through and all over a holly tree. Again, in the Home Wood, there is a fine collection of very well-grown rare and tender rhododendrons, some splendid magnolias, eucryphias, lomatias, and other unusual exotics. In that part of the park called the Avenue Ground the most striking of the flowering plants are the big-leaved rhododendrons, notably *sinogrande* and the handsome *R. falconeri*.

May and September are, in my experience, the best months in which to visit this garden, and at least two days should be allowed for the visit, more if possible.

12

Mount Stewart

The principal maker of the very remarkable gardens of Mount Stewart in County Down was the Marchioness of Londonderry, and as the work was not started until 1921, the gardens are not yet fifty years old. When one visits this garden it is very difficult to believe that it is so young, but there is a good explanation for its look of maturity: the soil and climate are favourable to the rapid growth of all kinds of plants.

In her foreword to the National Trust's handbook on these gardens, Lady Londonderry has this to say of the history of the house and grounds:

"Hugh Montgomery, Earl of Mount Alexander, sold the manor and property of Newtownards in 1675 to Robert Colville of Mount Colville, County Antrim. He also sold him the Templecrone Estate at the same time. These estates were later purchased by Alexander Stewart of Ballylawn Castle and Stewart's Court, County Donegal, in 1744. The Templecrone Estate is now merged in the present Mount Stewart demesne, but it is the old and correct name for this locality. When the property was bought from the Colvilles by Alexander Stewart, it was called Mount Pleasant, whether in reference to a house built here before Mount Stewart we do not know. Alexander was responsible for building the old and beautiful west end part of the house, in the Adam style.

"When my husband and I first came here on a visit for him to recuperate from appendicitis, some time before he succeeded to the property, I thought the house and surroundings were the dampest, darkest and saddest place I had ever stayed in, in the winter. Large ilex trees almost touched the house in places, and sundry other big trees almost blocked out the light and air."

The Marquis of Londonderry here in question succeeded to the property in 1915 and

Mount Stewart, where a richly planted formal garden is set in a wild garden in a manner reminiscent of Italian Baroque gardens.

lent the house to the government as a convalescent hospital for wounded soldiers. But in 1921 the Marquis and Marchioness of Londonderry went to live at Mount Stewart. And Lady Londonderry says that the gardens as we now have them would never have been made at all but for the fact that her husband resigned his office in the British Government to become Minister of Education in the first Ulster Parliament in 1921, a post which he held for five years. Moreover, another quite fortuitous circumstance contributed to the making of these gardens:

> "During the difficult period of demobilisation on a vast scale and pending the reabsorption of men into industry, the Ulster Landlords were asked to employ as many extra labourers as possible. At least twenty were allocated to Mount Stewart. This, then, was the opportunity to plan and make the grounds surrounding the house not only more cheerful and liveable, but beautiful as well."

Lady Londonderry's experience of gardening had until then been confined to gardens in the coldest parts of England and the far north of Scotland. In County Down she soon discovered that the mild climate, produced by the Gulf Stream virtually sweeping the shores of that part of Ireland, the relatively low rainfall compensated for by very high atmospheric humidity, and the relatively high figure of sunshine hours, meant that sub-tropical plants could be grown at Mount Stewart. Under the influence of two great gardening mentors, Sir John Ross, of the famous Rostrevor Garden, now alas no more, and Sir Herbert Maxwell, of Montreith in Wigtownshire, she made up her mind to take full advantage of these special conditions. But her gardening was never dominated by plantsmanship, and Mount Stewart is very much a designed, a formal, garden in all but its strictly woodland parts. In some respects, indeed, it is almost a baroque garden, so much formal ornament of one kind and another is there, and I have heard it criticised as "fussy". The reader will judge for himself from the pictures we use here whether this is or is not the case. To me, the important achievement at Mount Stewart is that of using exotic plants within a formal setting in which all the styles discussed in the first chapter of this book are to be found, integrated into a successful whole.

In describing the gardens I shall take advantage of the National Trust handbook to get the many enclosures into some sort of order; but of my own knowledge of the garden for the rest.

At the point where visitors enter the gardens, the Clay Gates, one of the most striking features of the formal parts of these gardens is to be seen, the tall, clipped evergreen arches enclosing a paved walk. The idea is taken from some Spanish gardens, but it is very unfortunate that the species chosen as material in which to carry it out was *Cupressus macrocarpa*. In theory this was a good idea, for this is a fast-growing cypress and would enable the

The Monterey cypress arcades at Mount Stewart give this garden its unique character.

gardener to accomplish the final result very quickly. It was probably not realised in 1921 that the foliage of this cypress dies back at the base as the tree grows. A number of these very handsome arches have, therefore, died back and are having to be replanted. Nevertheless, there is nothing like them in any other Irish or British garden.

After this *macrocarpa* walk comes the Mairi Garden. This is a stone garden in the shape of a Tudor Rose and planted to white and blue plants, and centred on a fountain decorated by the figure of a child in lead, the "Mairi, Mairi, Quite Contrary" of the nursery rhyme. The plants are chiefly madonna lilies, white crinums and agapanthus; for my own taste this garden would be better planted with smaller-flowered, more delicate species, and we have here a case of plantsmanship rather overwhelming the sense of fitness in design. However, the Mairi garden is a very striking sight when in full flower. A summerhouse with a dove-cote, and a pergola walk planted to the scented, white-flowered rhododendron species of the *maddenii* series, complete this garden. Among its remarkable shrubs and trees, however, is an enormous *Fuchsia excorticata*, a *Eucalyptus viminalis* and a handsome *Pittosporum eugenoides*. There is also a specimen of the palm *Cordyline australis* which seems to me out of place in that setting.

One of the features of Mount Stewart is fantastic statuary of more or less fabulous beasts—a return, this, to the taste of the seventeenth century and Jacobean gardens—in stone and in topiary. For my taste there is a good deal too much of this; the first examples which the visitor comes to are the dodos on pillars at the way into the Mairi Garden and out of it into the so-called Dodo Garden, which has some very interesting plants, notably a good *Magnolia watsonii* and some plants of *Lapageria rosea*, a Chilean climber with very beautiful waxy, pendent, rose-pink flowers, and a good, fragrant form of *Rhododendron decorum*.

These two minor gardens are followed by one of the principal ones, the Italian Garden. Here is what the Marchioness of Londonderry has to say about this:

"The Italian garden, which faces south, runs the entire length of the garden. It is a hundred yards by fifty. The general idea of the stonework was taken from the Villa Gamberaia, near Florence in Italy, also from the Villa Farnese at Caprarola and adapted to the site. The design of the beds in the centre of the garden was adapted on a modified scale from one of the gardens at Dunrobin Castle, Sutherland, the home of the writer's mother. The design at Mount Stewart was duplicated—an eastern parterre and a western one, with a wide lawn down the centre, planted on either side by *Cordyline australis*. The levelling of the garden commenced in the spring of 1919 and the retaining walls in winter. All the work was done by local men—an old stonemason who was a great craftsman made all the stone walls every-

Mount Stewart. The garden at Mount Stewart, created by the Marchioness of Londonderry, is a remarkable example of how a grand garden can be planted and brought to maturity well within a single lifetime. The garden shows the influence of every major gardening style in the history of the art.

A touch of comedy in the statuary, which is a feature of Mount Stewart.

where in the garden. He also erected the Gazebos at Tir N'an Oge. By name Joe Girvan, he was a native of Greyabbey. The other craftsman connected with the gardens was a real artist, Thomas Beattie: he was a Newtownards man. . . . He built the balustrades and made all the animals—the parapets and the tall monkeypot pillars and the large pots, also the Summer House in the Mairi Garden, and all the piers and finials. I supplied him with the designs and dimensions."

This part of the garden is rich in exotic plants. I shall not list them all, but among them are crinodendrons, *Abutilon vitifolium*, some interesting cestrums, abelias, a *Beschorneria yuccoides*, and the loveliest of the clematis, *C. indivisa*. Callistemon, metrosideros and freemontia are also represented, and two of the tenderest and best of the buddleias. On the upper terrace, right by the house and using the pillars of the portico, there is a collection of the Banksian rose varieties.

Immediately below the Italian Garden and reached by a flight of circular steps, is the so-called Spanish Garden which takes its name from the Spanish-tiled roof of its pavilion which is also tiled inside, but the tiles of the interior came from Palestine.

Topiary in yew, cypress and box is a feature of Mount Stewart. The Irish harp beyond the Red Hand of Ulster planted into the paving.

Lady Londonderry says that this garden was based on the design of the Adam ceilings in the Mansion House. For me this is the most charming and successful of the gardens at Mount Stewart, and although it, too, has its quota of rare and tender exotics, the most beautiful plants to be seen in it are surely the moutans. It is remarkable that these tree-paeonies do so well in a garden so rich in rhododendrons.

Between these parts of the gardens and the wild or woodland garden there is another enclosed garden remarkable for the material of its hedges: the Peace Garden, so-called because it was used as a pets' cemetery, has one hedge of the Chilean *Drimys aromatica*, a shrub which is remarkably at home in the gardens of Northern Ireland and South-west Scotland, in some of which it seeds itself—most notably at Crarae. It has the richly-scented leaves of all the *Myrtaceae* and bright red young stems. The other unusual hedge is of the holly-like Chilean *Desfontainea spinosa*, which is always striking when in flower and covered with its tubular, orange blooms. Mount Stewart is remarkable for fine eucalyptus, and one of the best specimens, an *E. globulus*, grows at this point in the gardens.

The first part of the Wild Garden is the Lily Wood. As you go into this you pass a wall planted with the very tender rhododendrons which, in England, are grown under glass, including *R. edgeworthii*. More rhododendrons make the under-storey of the wood, although some of them are trees in their own right, among them the rare, pink-flowered form of *R. grande*. There are also eucryphias and embothriums and nothofagus. The lilies from which this part of the gardens takes its name are for the most part *L. martagon* var. *album* and *L. auratum* var. *platyphyllum*. As well as lilies, the wood is planted more than one species of the blue-flowered mecanopses, the best being Prain's form of *M. grandis*, hydrangeas allowed to grow naturally, *Cardiocrinum giganteum* and the cinnamon-barked *Myrtus luma*.

One returns to formalities, by way of a small rock-garden, in the Shamrock Garden. This is a paved garden in the shape of a shamrock leaf, enclosed in a twelve-foot hedge of *Cupressus macrocarpa*. In the centre of this garden, cut into the paving, is a bed in the shape of the Bloody Hand of Ulster, and this is planted to a dwarf heath; at least, it was when I saw it, although formerly the plant used was, apparently, *Iresine herbstii*, which has red leaves. The Hand is the crest of the McDonnells of Antrim: when the Scottish clans raced across the sea to Ulster, the land to be the winner's prize, the then McDonnell, seeing himself losing by a few yards, cut off his hand and threw it ahead on to the shore, and claimed the land. The top of the macrocarpa hedge is cut into some very fantastic topiary depicting a family hunting scene, the design being from the Psalter of Queen Mary Tudor. Another piece of elaborate topiary in this garden is a yew clipped into the shape of an Irish harp.

To the west of the house is the Sunk Garden and Pergola Garden. Three terraces descend to the sunk centre of this garden, which is also contained in tall macrocarpa hedges on three sides. The first of the terraces has a border or hedge of flame-red azaleas which

Mount Stewart. The use of masonry and fabulous beasts gives a firm skeleton to this great romantic garden.

Topiary animals dominate one of the formal courtyards of Mount Stewart.

I found too overwhelming for the scale of the planting. The centre of the sunk garden has four rectangular beds in low-clipped hedges of bay laurel. The beds have a fine show of some perennials, chiefly delphinium, and there are some interesting exotics in this part, as in all parts of Mount Stewart gardens: *Jovellana violacea* is by far the most attractive, but *Mitraria coccinea* is very striking in flower and so is the romneya-like but yellow-flowered *Dendromecon rigidum*.

A very effective part of the Wild Gardens, connecting the rest with the area known as the Lake Walk, is known as The Drive. On one side of it is a steep bank topped by some immense and ancient *Quercus ilex*, evergreen oaks, and by some enormous tree-heathers which really are trees with massive trunks. I have never seen these in flower, but the sight and scent of them must be remarkable. There is an interesting collection of conifers in this part of the garden, and a fine planting of the giant-leaved *Rhododendron macabeanum*, as

Detail of the tiling in the Spanish pavilion of the sunk garden at Mount Stewart.

well as other good members of the same genus, including the superlative hybrid "Penjerrick" and the August-flowering *R. auriculatum*. Perhaps the most remarkable plant of this region of the gardens is a climber from China, *Actinidia chinensis*, which I have not seen elsewhere: it climbs a sixty-foot robinia to the summit, and in midsummer is covered with one-inch apricot-scented flowers of bright yellow. From the Drive you turn into the Lake Walk which, as its name makes clear, is a walk beside the Mount Stewart lake, quite a large sheet of water. The way is planted richly with magnolias, rhododendrons, and other trees and shrubs, and with *Cardiocrinum giganteum*, *Lilium auratum*, and beyond, with some fine red-leaved maples. The most interesting tree of this Lake Walk part is, perhaps, the Chilean *Weinmannia trichosperma*.

There are other and more remote parts of this garden to be visited, but enough has been said to make it clear that Mount Stewart is as remarkable for diversity of styles represented as for the richness and variety of its plant material.

13

Castlewellan

This book confines itself to the representative pick of the Irish gardens, and among the best of those, as I have tried to show in Chapter 3, is Annes Grove in County Cork. That garden which is, for me at all events, the best in the North of Ireland is another Annesley garden, Castlewellan, the owner and gardener being Mr Gerald Annesley.

Castlewellan is near Newcastle in County Down. The whole region is botanically interesting, lying between an area of sand dunes between the inland and the sea, and the Mourne Mountains. The castle itself was built in 1856 and stands on a height, commanding very fine views over the park and a large lake to the mountains and to the sea. The building material is a warm, grey stone and it provides a good foil for the lawns and clipped golden yews in the immediate neighbourhood of the house. The soil is a light, acid gravel. Writing of the nature of the site from the horticultural point of view, in 1902, the fifth Earl Annesley, the first maker of this garden, said (R.H.S. *Journal*, Vol. 27):

"The garden is on one of the foothills of the Mourne Mountains in the County of Down, about three miles from the Irish Channel, thus benefiting from the mild influence of the gulf stream: it faces east and south and is surrounded by old forest trees, so that it is well sheltered. We suffer little from frost; ten degrees is the average; once, in the hard winter of 1895, we had fifteen degrees. The rainfall is about thirty-two inches; the subsoil is gravel, and as it lies on rather a steep hill there is perfect drainage—a great advantage for tender, as indeed it is for all, plants."

Hugh, the fifth Earl Annesley, who wrote this note, began his work as gardener of Castlewellan in about 1870, so that the gardens and collection of trees is just under a century old. The famous nursery firm of Veitch, then at its zenith, as well as other firms,

Castlewellan. In late Summer and early Autumn the eucryphia avenue is a unique feature.

collected rare plants for him, and he was thus responsible for new introductions, chiefly from the Far East. His son and successor, Francis, the sixth Earl, continued his father's work but employed the then flourishing Daisy Hill Nurseries at Newry. When Francis was killed while flying in 1914, Castlewellan was inherited by his sister, Lady Mabel Annesley. She, too, continued to collect and plant exotics and so, finally, did her son, Mr Gerald Annesley, who is still doing so.

The gardens of Castlewellan have a formal nucleus at the centre of a great parkland garden planted with a collection of trees, many of which are as rare and interesting as they are all remarkably well grown. The hilly form of the garden and park site is in itself very pleasing, and from the garden's highest ballustraded terrace, backed by the greenhouses and propagating frames in their own walled area, one gets glimpses of the sea between the heads of trees. The climate of the County Down littoral is very mild, and Lord Annesley's figure of ten degrees of frost in an average year is, I think, rather on the high side; in some years there is virtually no frost, and even in such savage winters as that of 1962/3 it is not nearly as bad as it is in most other parts of Britain. One hardly needs thermometer readings to be sure of this: a walk round the gardens, or round the neighbouring Slieve Donard nursery, identifying southern hemisphere plants which are notoriously tender, is evidence enough.

Central to the garden is the large walled "kitchen-garden" typical of Irish gardens of the period and by no means confined to the growing of vegetables. Its principal gate has a great *Eucalyptus urnigera* on one side and another gum, *E. cordata*, on the other. The garden slopes to the south, and is divided by a broad walk flanked by herbaceous borders backed by clipped hedges. The main walk is crossed at right angles by another pathway, so that this garden is composed of four rectangular areas, and at the crossway is a great stone vase. Some of the hedges are remarkable: they are composed of *Drimys aromatica*, which I have mentioned as flourishing in other Irish gardens, although it is a more or less tender Chilean plant. Its dense, neat growth makes an admirable hedge where it can be grown, and as its young growth is not green but greenish bronze, such a hedge is particularly handsome in the spring and early summer. The walled garden is decorated with Irish Yews at regular intervals and these are kept trimmed. As, again as in many Irish gardens, these yews are grown through by the perennial climbing "nasturtium". *Tropaeoleum speciosum*, they are strangely decorated in season with streaks and patches of flame red.

One of the great beauties of Castlewellan is its vistas down straight paths, through handsome gateways in walls, focused on the great basins which mark the crossways. Describing part of what he had seen there in the R.H.S. *Journal* (Part Six, Vol. LXXV), Mr Graham Thomas was much struck with this aspect:

Castlewellan. Touches of formal Italianate gardening are set into this great romantic garden of trees and flowering shrubs.

"Looking along this remarkable walk to the central vase, we had the striking picture of the white tiers of *Viburnum tomentosum* 'Mariesii', against the tall forms of conifers blue, green and golden. Amongst them towers a fine specimen of *Pinus sylvestris aurea*, forty-three feet high with a good crown, the hybrid *Cupressus leylandii*, thirty-eight feet high, *Libocedrus decurrens* and *chilensis*, *Pinus parviflora glauca*, *P. montezumae hertwegii* and many others; *Drimys winteri* in full flower (thirty-one feet), *Myrtus luma* and *Pittosporums*. Two trees with beautiful bark were *Arbutus menziesii*, thirty feet, and a young fastigiate specimen of *Betula papyrifera*. These are all in the two rectangles on the left of the central walk."

Mr Thomas then goes on to describe another of the formal vistas of this beautifully planted garden, a garden in which the expert plantsmanship of Lord Annesley and his successors has never been allowed to take too much precedence of design but has been skilfully subordinated to it. He then makes a point which also struck me very forcibly when I first saw this garden:

"Most of the planting in this garden was carried out by the fifth Earl Annesley, and it was presumably his desire to grow the cypresses each with many stems. The resulting immense pyramidal thickets of *Thujas* or *Cupressus* are certainly impressive to a degree, though possibly dangerous in old age. The specimens include *Picea breweriana*, nineteen feet, *P. smithiana*, *P. morrisonicola; Abies amabilis*, *A. concolor wattezii*, *A. georgei; Cephalotaxus drupacea; Arthrotaxis; Glyptostrobus heterophyllus; Dacridium, Podocarpus*, etc."

What Mr Thomas did not note here is that Lord Annesley treated such giants as Wellingtonia, the enormous Californian Redwood, in the same way, creating thereby magnificent spectacles of multiple trunks which are a fascinating feature of this great garden.

Not only does design predominate in the placing of the trees and shrubs relative to the shape of the whole planting, but in the pleasing associations of one kind of foliage with another: here is Mr Thomas on the subject:

"Long cross-vistas and a curved walk round the enclosing walls bring to light the great variety of form and foliage in this collection. The contrast at one point of an exceptionally tall weeping ash, the broad-leaved *Cordyline indivisa*, and the feathery grace of the *Juniperus recurva* was particularly noticeable. At another point a pyramid of golden-green *Thuja plicata variegata (zebrina)* is placed next to *Acer palmatum atropurpureum*, nineteen feet high and about thirty-five feet across.

The scientific importance of the tree collection in the park of Castlewellan is not allowed to overshadow style and design in lay-out.

The top path has a formal decoration of clipped Portuguese laurels on stems — and wide borders along the walls contain many sun-loving shrubs such as hoherias, cestrums, ceanothus, *Corokia cotoneaster,* leptospermums, nandinas, feijoa, and *Cornus capitata.* . . .''

One of the most remarkable features of Castlewellan does not appear in Mr Thomas's necessarily brief account because he was not there in the late summer. From the bottom of the steps which lead down from the high terrace, to the walk round the walls already mentioned, there is a double avenue of eucryphias which is surely unique. The outside rank is formed of *Eucryphia cordifolia* whose entire leaves are less graceful than those of the other species, but whose large and beautifully cupped flowers with great golden centres are the finest in the genus and are, moreover, borne in enormous numbers; the inner ranks include *Eucryphia gluttinosa, E. billardieri (lucida), E. moorei, E.* x *intermedia* and, I think, either *E.* x 'Nymansensis' or the Mount Usher version of the same cross. There are both single and double-flowered forms of the hybrids. The mass of white flower in late summer and early autumn is astonishing and the meaning of the words "bee-loud" becomes very clear, for honey-bees love all the eucryphias.

Being, alas, ignorant in the matter of conifers, of the collection of all the genera of these I can say only that the trees are among the most beautiful I have seen anywhere and that among them are many rarities. There are a number of species of eucalypts very well grown and this is the only garden in north-west Europe where I have seen the blue-gum in flower. Among the trees and shrubs which I noted as especially interesting or especially handsome, in the park, are the following.

Sophora tetraptera, the Kowhai of New Zealand, is a tall tree and flowers very freely, not on a wall but free standing and protected only by other trees. You can see this flowering tree in some Cornish and even Devon gardens, but as a rule it seems only to flower on walls there. The most lovely broad-leaved and evergreen silver tree I have seen anywhere is at Castlewellan, and enormous specimen of *Pittosporum eugenoides argentea-variegata.* The leaves of this tree should be examined in detail: they are zoned, the inner zone being a greenish pewter in colour, and the marginal zone silver-cream. The whole effect, in bright sunshine, is magnificent. As in all good Irish gardens there are well-grown specimens of Embothrium and they are here used with the discretion called for by their flaming scarlet flowers; and some good Acacias, including the florist's "mimosa". There are several, but one notably fine, specimens of what is, for me, the most fascinating of all coloured foliage shrubs, and the most interesting of the genus *Drimys, D. colorata.* This is very rare in English gardens and by no means common in Irish ones. The base colour of the leaves is golden-yellow, but they are shot, speckled and margined with garnet-red.

Castlewellan is remarkable for beautifully contrived vistas framed in fine gateways.

Castlewellan in September. The eucryphia avenue in flower.

But details of the plants of especial interest to be found in a garden, while some must be given, do very little if anything to convey an idea of what the garden is like. The particular excellencies of Castlewellan are two. One: the placing of the many exotic trees, shrubs and other plants is such that the idea "botanical collection" does not, as one wanders in this garden, enter one's head. Native and exotic plants have been used as material in the making of a horticultural work of art, and not planted simply for their own sake. The same spirit is apparent in the treatment of the conifers, that creation of thickets rather than specimens which Mr Thomas refers to. In the second place the balance between foliage colour and form, and flower colour and form, is exactly what, in my opinion, it ought to be. It is true that Castlewellan can do without a lot of flower, for very few gardens have so much variety and colour in the foliage of their plants. There is enough flower at Castlewellan to give the garden liveliness but never so much as to overwhelm the foliage and produce that "riot of colour" effect which is so offensive in the soft Irish setting.

Castlewellan is, in short, a picturesque garden in the literal sense of the adjective, that is, a work of art.

143

14

Glasnevin

Ireland has, of course, its own Botanic Gardens and they, and their curators and staff, have played an important part in the improvement of the Irish Garden. We have noted, for example, how Sir F. W. Moore, who became Curator in 1879 in succession to his father, helped and advised the Walpoles in the creation of Mount Usher.

In 1790 the Right Honourable Dublin Society passed a resolution to start a Botanic Garden, "for promoting scientific knowledge in the various branches of agriculture and planting as well as to foster a taste for practical and scientific botany". As a result the Botanic Gardens, Glasnevin, Dublin, were founded and endowed by the Irish Parliament. From the beginning, and although the gardens were controlled by the Dublin Society until 1880, they were financed by, at first in part and later altogether, the nation, Parliament making a series of annual grants beginning with one of £300 — say about £6,000 in modern values — in 1790.

Who was the prime mover in this undertaking? The "Foster" referred to in the following extract from the *Dublin Magazine* for 1800 was the Speaker of the Irish Parliament and, later, Lord Oriel:

"In the planning and executing of this garden it has been uncommonly fortunate that the abilities and assistance of the first-rate character which this nation or any other can boast of, were most condescendingly and arduously exerted to further this great national object, and while the name of Foster remains respected and beloved by every Irishman, so long will this garden perpetuate the taste and abilities of this great and good man."

The site of the gardens, twenty-seven acres of light loam over gravel of which Mr J. W. Besant, Keeper of the Gardens, wrote that "a poorer soil or one less likely to produce good

Horticultural beauty and charm are by no means forgotten at the National Botanic Garden, Glasnevin, Dublin, although scientific economic botany takes precedence.

results could scarcely have been found" was bought in 1795, but work had begun before that, for the site had been leased for some years.

Display and trial beds were made, paths laid out, greenhouses built during the early years, and progress must have been swift because the gardens had already, in the first decades of the nineteenth century, become famous for their collection of Cape Heaths— 150 species—under glass. There was a Cattle Garden for trials of fodder plants; an Esculent Garden with vegetables useful to man; a Dyers' Garden for the trial of dye-producing plants; a Hay Garden for the study of hay-making plants; a Nursery; a Grass Garden; a Medicinal Garden and a Hibernian Garden. The first decades of the nineteenth century were dominated at Glasnevin by the famous botanist Dr Wade. He died in 1825, and Dr Samuel Litton became the Glasnevin Professor of Botany. Large changes and modernisations were under-taken when, in 1830, Underwood, curator for thirty-six years, made way for a younger man, Ninian Niven, who was a skilful landscape gardener as well as a good botanist. He had made his name by laying out and planting the Great Phoenix Park landscape garden. In their general shape, quite considerable areas of the Glasnevin gardens are still as Niven layed them out in his remodelling of the whole place. Niven started the work of training young men to be professional gardeners which has continued ever since.

In 1838 Niven was succeeded by David Moore who had until then been assistant curator of the Trinity College Botanic Garden at Ballsbridge. Moore continued Niven's policy, but undertook new work on his own account, notably in pulling down the old hot-houses and replacing them with new curvilinear iron ones built by Turner of Dublin, builder of the large Palm House at Kew, and financed by Parliament and the Dublin Society. The gardens began to make a more important contribution to academic scientific work at this time. In his short account of this Mr J. W. Besant says:

"Dr Litton, the society's botanist, died in 1845, and was succeeded by Dr Harvey, a native of Limerick, who had travelled extensively and was apparently interested in botanical science, the actual work of the gardens being carried out by the curator. The Society's Botanist had up to this delivered a certain number of botanical lectures in the gardens, and some at the society's house in Kildare Street. In 1854, however, the Government made a change, stopping the lectures at the gardens and transferring them to the College of Science, where they were delivered by the Professor of Botany, who then, as now, brought his class to the gardens for occasional demonstrations. All the plant material required for teaching purposes in the college was supplied from the gardens, as well as material required in the School of Art. These arrangements continue, but many more specimens are now supplied to technical schools, colleges, etc." ("Botanic Gardens: Origin, History

Glasnevin is the National Botanic Garden of the Irish Republic in a Dublin suburb.

and Development", *Department of Agriculture Journal*, Vol. XXXIII, No. 2, Dublin, 1935.)

Like all botanical gardens Glasnevin found itself constantly needing new greenhouses and hothouses. The Victoria Regia House, named for the great Amazon water-lily which was grown there, was built in 1854 and large extensions to the Palm House were finished in 1862. In 1883 there were autumn gales of such violence that this range of buildings was severely damaged, and a new and larger one was built over it in the following year.

The curatorship of the first Dr Moore was a long one, forty-one years. His successor, Mr (later Sir) F. W. Moore, whose widow still has one of the prettiest and most interesting small gardens in Ireland, very soon added twelve acres to the thirty-one which he took over. This new ground was planted to become the West Arboretum. F. W. Moore's policy was one of renewal, and a great deal of second-rate material was grubbed up and replaced by better and more interesting trees and shrubs. Moore was keeper—the title curator had been superseded—for the same term as his father or a little longer, forty-two years, for, having been knighted in 1910 and being recognised as one of the half-dozen greatest scientific gardeners then living, he retired in 1922 to be succeeded by Mr J. W. Besant, who continued the policy of improving and extending the plant collections and had the task of getting a quart into a pint pot because there was now no further room for territorial expansion. Under Mr Besant's rule, and that of his successor the present keeper, Dr Walsh, the Rock Garden was enlarged and rebuilt, the former Willow Garden was planted to conifers and rhododendrons, a Water Garden made along the banks of the River Tolka, and various other works of improvement carried out, many of them designed to make better use of the limited amount of space available.

The first division of the Glasnevin Gardens immediately inside the gates is a shrubbery, separated from the path by a border used for the growing of early flowering perennials. On the other side of the path is a good collection of herbaceous perennials. This path leads to the Tree Fern House, which has a fine collection of dicksonias, cyatheas and other tree ferns, as well as many species of ground ferns and a very interesting display of Filmy Ferns including the famous "Killarney Fern". The next house in the range is the Victoria Regia House, where the giant water-lily from the Amazon flowers every year in the central tank, lesser tropical water lilies in the side tanks. After that, and in sharp contrast, comes a house full of arid-soil succulents and cacti, one of the best collections of them I have seen anywhere.

The next range of greenhouses is called the Curvilinear Range, and is the one which was built in 1843. It consists of a Cool House, where many plants which are only just not hardy, and which often grow perfectly well out of doors in the south-west of Ireland, are

Five minutes from the centre of Dublin, one of the views from the National Botanic Garden, Glasnevin.

Fine specimen trees, as well as botanical collections, make the National Botanic Garden, Glasnevin, as beautiful as it is scientifically important.

housed; the tall central section, with a collection of tender conifers and some banksias; and the Stove which, among other tropical plants, contains a good collection of bromeliads and specimens of such economic plants of the tropics as coffee, cocoa and sugar cane.

The Orchid Houses are separate from the other ranges of greenhouses, and the collection of orchids is a good one; it was, at one time, among the best in the world; whether this is still the case I am not competent to judge. One curious fact connected with the Orchid Houses: in their entrance porch was housed a small collection of sarracenias, the North American Pitcher Plants, and as a consequence, apparently of their semi-exposure, some of the species have established themselves and become naturalised in a bog in Roscommon.

There are two other important greenhouses: the Palm House which is seventy feet tall and contains a very fine collection of plants both economic and otherwise, some giant bamboos, cyads and giant ferns. And then, the Camellia House, less important for camellias which are in any case all hardy in Ireland, than for its displays of flowering plants in summer and notably for its display of many species of begonias.

Glasnevin. An Umbrella pine dominates the beautifully planted rock garden.

One of the National Botanic Garden walks, where collections of herbaceous perennials are backed by shrubs and trees.

There would be no point in describing divisions of the garden whose name describes them: there are, for example, the Herbaceous Walk, the Rock Garden, the Bamboo Walk, the River Walk. It should be said, however, that even where the principal purpose of the authorities is to display a particular genus for botanical and educational reasons, ornamental gardening is practised by, for example, underplanting with daffodils and snowdrops, so that even for the non-technical visitor the gardens are very pleasant.

The area of the gardens known as the Mill Race, once a willow collection, but ruined by flooding, was recovered and raised during the keepership of Mr Besant, and planted with conifers and rhododendrons. The banks of the river at this point have been used for a good collection of primulas, meconopsis and other moisture-loving plants. The River Walk itself lies between the tolka and the pond. The pond is rich in aquatic plants in great variety, from the spectacular water-lilies to the more modest species, and its margins have been made into a very well-stocked Bog Garden.

An example of clever formal planting with succulents at the National Botanic Garden, where models of all modern garden styles can be seen.

Glasnevin includes a good Pinetum and, in the West Arboretum, an interesting and well-grown collection of maples and of many other genera of broad-leaved trees; there are also collections of ivies, a relatively new collection of oaks, and a collection of all the different kinds of yews.

The Vine Border Walk is a division of the gardens which I found rich in useful lessons for the ordinary gardener. There is a wall with a good collection of climbing and scandent plants; a Crocus collection; an Iris collection of the May and June flowering kinds; a *Paeonia* collection confined to the botanical species and, for autumn visitors, a Michaelmas Daisy collection. Other collections beyond this area and on the way back to the Curvilinear Range of greenhouses, are the Chinese Shrubs; the Leguminous Shrubs; the Magnolias; the species roses; the *Prunus;* the *Pyrus;* and the *Syringa.*

Apart from the scientific and educational work done by Glasnevin, especially on the economic plants, the gardens are, then, of great value to ornamental horticulture, providing a permanent object-lesson for gardeners and thus contributing continuously to the improvement of the Irish garden.

15

The Irish Garden

My own taste, knowledge of the gardens in question, and to some extent convenience, have had much to do with the choice of the gardens which I have used to represent the Irish garden; but I believe that the choice is vindicated by the quality and the significance of the gardens displayed in the foregoing chapters.

Mount Usher was made, as described, under the influence of William Robinson, the great Irish gardener who dominated horticultural style from about 1870 until the end of the century or rather longer, whose influence, indeed, continued beyond his lifetime and still continues. The climate and the soil of the Irish littoral is very favourable to the creation of natural or Robinsonian gardens, and to the use of a wider and richer range of exotic plants than would be possible elsewhere in the same latitude. At Mount Usher five generations of one family have practised gardening in this same style; it is no wonder that the style therefore finds its superlative expression in this great garden. To quote Mr Lanning Roper once again:

> "It is the mixture of the exotic with the natural freshness and greenness that makes the gardens of the British Isles so far more satisfying than the gardens of the Mediterranean or the Tropics. . . ."

And in Ireland this mixture, which I have elsewhere called the "paradise" garden, since it is a harking back to the ideal of pre-Fall perfection by the bringing and associating together of the most beautiful plants from the five continents, the style is to be seen at its best if only because the "natural freshness and greenness" are superlative and the conditions such that the "exotic" can be represented at its most impressive.

In Annes Grove and in Castlewellan, at opposite extremes of the country, Ireland has two gardens which represent not pure paradise gardening, but a perfectly accomplished mingling of natural and formal styles. In the case of Annes Grove the formal style is

One of the fountain basins at Castlewellan.

simple and unpretentious: it derives from the ideas about well-ordered gardening which were popularised by J. C. Loudon in the early nineteenth century, and there is no touch of grandeur. The formality of Castlewellan, on the other hand, while not in itself an expression of grandeur, has vestiges—for example in the great stone basins, the broad, straight vistas, the fine gateways and the *ronds points*—of the grand Roman Renaissance style. In both cases the formal garden is set in a natural, Robinsonian garden, but again there is an interesting difference of taste: at Annes Grove the note is one of romantic richness whereas at Castlewellan, despite its exotics, there is always, even in the park-like sections of the garden, a note of classical restraint.

Art was first used in the gardens of Christian Europe in the Humanist gardens of Tuscany, which linked our ornamental horticulture with that of the Hellenic, or at least the Hellenistic world, since Petrarch and his followers drew their inspiration and ideas from memories of the Roman garden. The style survives in the Irish garden, and notably at Glenveagh and Birr Castle. But Glenveagh, that remote far western garden on the very edge of Europe, also has representations of other styles and traditions—in fact of most of them excepting French Renaissance and English Landscape. And once again we have formal gardens, and in this case semi-formal gardens, set in a great paradise garden on Robinsonian lines.

At Fota, Ireland has a rather special case, an example of what one might call hibernised French. There is Gallic grandeur in the straight, broad walks, in the handsome stone-work, and, curiously enough, in the vistas of open grass and fine trees which, although like an English park, is somehow faintly reminiscent of Le Nôtre. The flatness of the site has been accepted and used instead of being merely put up with. But there is also a good example of the native Irish walled garden; and that very remarkable Fernery, a piece of eighteenth century romanticism carried out in exotic materials; in its mixed shrub and perennial borders this garden has, too, a good example of modern gardening.

Modern gardening on two different levels, and evidence for the vitality of Irish gardening in our time are to be found in Ardsallagh and Mount Congreve. Ardsallagh is firmly designed without being formal. The choice of plant material has been influenced by clever plantsmanship as well as by soil and climate, but these have not been allowed to overwhelm the consideration of design, and the garden is not a collection of plants, but an integral work of art. It is, indeed, a model of what the twentieth century garden of the medium to large kind should be: it takes full advantage of soil and climate but never without a proper regard for art.

As for Mount Congreve, a pessimist might claim that what Mr Ambrose Congreve is doing there is something which can have no significance for modern Irish gardening in general, or, indeed, for modern gardening anywhere. But I do not myself believe that the

A view of the terrace at Powerscourt.

great romantic garden, in which a lavish use of exotic flowering trees and shrubs is permissible where the scale is large enough, is doomed. It may well be true that there are few private gardeners who would do such work nowadays; and that there will, in future, be even fewer. But institutions can and perhaps will do what private citizens cannot. For example, modern municipal gardening in England shows, at its best, the influence of the great private gardens, and there is no reason why this should not be so also in Ireland. Mr Congreve is setting an example which will not, perhaps, be followed by many Irishmen in their private gardens: it is a matter of being able to afford it. But Irish industry and municipalities may learn from him how to embellish the surroundings of the places where men and women work and play.

In Ilnacullin, Ireland has a garden unique in the world. Made by a man steeped in the culture of Renaissance Italy and with a great love of the architectural Italian gardens, for a patron rich enough to carry out the artist's vision and who was himself under the influence of the prevailing taste among his friends for Robinsonian gardening and the planting of exotics "after Nature", this garden on Garinish Island is a perfectly accomplished mixture of the Italianate, the Landscape and the Romantic garden. I call it unique because the dreamlike beauty of the surrounding country and the extraordinary climate of south-west Ireland together give it a beauty and a distinction, in the setting and in the magnificent growth of its exotic plants, which no artifice could have ensured.

Coming to Powerscourt, Ireland has on the one hand a native version of that grand, ennobling style which was given its first expression in the villas and palaces of Renaissance Rome, and, on the other hand, an outstandingly beautiful example of landscape gardening. And this, moreover, when we come down from taking long views, to close-ups, is enriched by detail nearly all of which is admirable, for example in the planting into the parklike woodland walks of flowering exotics. The garden shows above all how Ireland can, when she will, not only make the traditions of European art her own, but combine them in a fashion peculiar to herself.

Birr Castle is a horticultural masterpiece created within a single generation, although in an older park, by two master gardeners. It reflects a thorough knowledge of all the major traditions in European garden art, but its representations of a number of the traditional styles are not copies but original works. This is, of all the Irish gardens known to me, the one in which both thought and taste are most apparent, and it is in this respect a permanent object lesson for the gardeners of all Ireland. There they can see how flower colours can best be associated together, and how the beauty of a planting can be enhanced by the correct juxtaposition of plants complementary to each other in form and habit. And this garden has another very great merit: in the softness of its lines and colours it fits into the Irish landscape without ever offending the eye by any incongruity between garden and setting.

Birr Castle from the lakeside.

In that respect Rowallane, although a superlative garden of its kind, is the antithesis of Birr Castle. At least it is in the famous Spring Garden. There, in May, the colour is over-whelming; the temptation to make a rich display of gorgeousness has been yielded to and all other considerations have been secondary. This is not, as it happens, much to my taste. But it is certainly a spectacular demonstration of what can be done in Irish conditions. And there can be no such criticism of the more formal parts of this garden, in which while the plant material is rich, the use of it is restrained by good rules of art.

Mount Stewart is the only Irish garden I know in which the Jacobean taste is revived in the stone and topiary ornament. But it is a protean garden, the number of styles which have influenced its maker is a constant source of surprise as is the manner in which exotic plants have been used in expressing them; the garden is thoroughly Irish in the wealth and range of its plant material and in the superlative growth of its trees and flowering shrubs.

I have said nothing about the small, private gardens of Ireland because the object of this book is to display garden art in Ireland and there, as in other countries, that is best represented in the great gardens. The Irish householder is not by any means such an enthusiastic gardener as his English opposite number: if he were, then, given the Irish climate, Ireland would surpass England as a land of small gardens. But at least this can be said: if the Irish, like the rest of us all over Europe, take to gardening their new residential and industrial estates, then they have in their great gardens in every province of their country the models, representative of every European tradition and style in garden art, which they will need.

Index